© Copyright 2023 – All rights reserved.

The content contained within this book may not be reproduced, duplicated or transmitted without direct written permission from the author or the publisher.

Under no circumstances will any blame or legal responsibility be held against the publisher, or author, for any damages, reparation, or monetary loss due to the information contained within this book, either directly or indirectly.

Legal Notice:

This book is copyright protected. It is only for personal use. You cannot amend, distribute, sell, use, quote or paraphrase any part, or the content within this book, without the consent of the author or publisher.

Disclaimer Notice:

Please note the information contained within this document is for educational and entertainment purposes only. All effort has been executed to present accurate, up to date, reliable, complete information. No warranties of any kind are declared or implied. Readers acknowledge that the author is not engaged in the rendering of legal, financial, medical or professional advice. The content within this book has been derived from various sources. Please consult a licensed professional before attempting any techniques outlined in this book.

By reading this document, the reader agrees that under no circumstances is the author responsible for any losses, direct or indirect, that are incurred as a result of the use of the information contained within this document, including, but not limited to, errors, omissions, or inaccuracies.

ISBN: 979-8-872-27947-1

Contents

Title Page	VI
Introduction	1
1. What is Self-Love?	5
The Concept of Self-Love	
Action Steps Towards Self-Love	
Self-Love Story You Need To Learn From Today	
Chapter Activity: Create Your Own Self-Love Journal!	
2. Boosting Your Self-Confidence	27
Reasons for Women's Low Self-Confidence	
The Concept of Self-Confidence	
How to Develop Self-Confidence	
Action Steps Towards Developing Self-Confidence	
Self-Confidence Story You Need To Learn From Today	
Chapter Activity: Set Your Own S.M.A.R.T Goals!	
3. Giving Your Body The Positivity It Needs	42
What Is Body Positivity?	
Deconstructing Diet Culture	
Understanding Societal Pressures Around Body Image	
Shapewear and Your Level of Body Positivity	
How To Be More Body Positive	
Body Positivity Story You Need To Learn From Today	

      Chapter Activity: Body Positivity Truth or Dare Game!

4. A Life Without Self-Consciousness   62
   Recognizing Self-Consciousness
   Overcoming Self-Doubt Once and for All
   How To Overcome Self-Doubt
   Overcoming Self-Doubt Story You Need To Learn From Today
   Chapter Activity: 'How Self-Conscious Are You?' Self-Assessment

5. Accepting Your Own History   79
   Understanding Childhood Trauma
   Tips for Healing Childhood Trauma
   Overcoming Childhood Trauma Story You Need To Learn From Today
   Chapter Activity: Healing Journal Prompts

6. Practicing Self-Compassion   93
   Understanding Self-Compassion
   Learning to Release Shame
   Self-Forgiveness
   Exercises for Practicing Self-Compassion
   Self-Compassion Story You Need To Learn From Today
   Chapter Activity: A Letter To Burn

7. The Way You Talk to Yourself   111
   Recognizing Negative Self-Talk
   Countering Negative Self-Talk
   Ways To Improve Self-Talk
   Self-Talk Story You Need to Learn from Today
   Chapter Activity: Change Your Vocabulary

8. Attaining the Ultimate Self-Joy   120
   Self-Understanding Is the Key to Happiness
   V.I.T.A.L.S of Happiness
   Finding Passion and Purpose
   Learning How to Prioritize Your Happiness

       Activities for Self-Joy
       Self-Joy Story You Need To Learn From Today
       Chapter Activity: Five Minutes of Joy Every Day

9. Conclusion   137

References   139

What If I Don't Love Me?

The Self-Love Knowledge Every Woman Needs to Relearn Self-Compassion, Regain Self-Confidence, and Reclaim Self-Joy

Paetyn Alexander

Little AP Publishing

Introduction

Do you ever feel like, as women, we have shame built into our systems? When we show our grief and cry in front of people, we say, "*I'm sorry, this is embarrassing.*" When we enter a room, we bow our heads and shrink ourselves, as if we won't fit the doorframe, or we would bother the crowded room by our mere presence. When we look at pictures after a fun or proud moment, we get a sinking feeling in our stomach as we immediately zoom into our insecurities: "*My arms look big here,*" "*Why do I smile like that,*" "*My stomach fat makes me look pregnant,*" and so on.

    The list of what we "should be" seems endless. Build a career, but don't just have a stable job, you have to be a "girlboss" too. Take care of your home, but it shouldn't just be clean and comfortable, it should look straight out of Architectural Digest as well. On top of that, be a loving mom, but not just any mom; be a cool mom, and don't forget to be a doting wife, but sexy—and also classy. Make time for exercising, eating healthy, getting your hair and nails done, shaving, waxing, or threading, having a nightly skincare routine, investing, improving yourself by enrolling in a class, and socializing with your family, in-laws, friends, co-workers, and your kids' friends' parents. Jeez! It's all so impossible, isn't it?

    It's like we're constantly walking on a tightrope, being motivated by the saying, "We can have it all!" And if you don't have it all, you start thinking that maybe *you* are the problem. I'm here to tell you upfront that, no, you are not the problem.

Something that could take years to realize is that this battle is something that could never be won by diligently ticking every checkbox. Truth is, all that leads to is one nagging feeling constantly imposed upon us, which if we don't learn to break away from could lead to us living inauthentic, unhappy lives. That feeling is this: You are not good enough.

When I was in sixth grade, my class went on a field trip to a ski hill. In order to rent skis, everyone's heights and weights needed to be measured. My teacher weighed each of us in front of the entire class—which, looking back, is such a horrible idea and gives you a lot of insight about him as an educator. When it was my turn to be weighed, he made the following comment: "Wow, that's a lot!"

The scale read 124 pounds. At over five feet tall, I was the tallest girl in class; in fact, taller than a lot of the boys. However, that didn't stop the class from laughing at what he said—laughing at *me*. This is my earliest memory of feeling shame at my body and who I was. This was the day I learned that I was not what I was supposed to be, and it would take decades to move past that shame. As a result, I was only 12 years old when I started dieting. My high school years were spent volleying between starving myself, overexercising, making myself physically sick, and binge eating. I spent years punishing myself for not being who I was supposed to be. Years of putting my opinions and desires second so as to make other people happy. Years of not saying "no," of being the easy-going person who got along with everyone for fear of having no one. Years of never speaking up believing my voice wasn't worth hearing. After a while, this just became who I was.

As a young adult, I was able to live "comfortably" in my body so long as I exercised most days and limited what I ate. I pushed myself to be this way. I got married, and I had two beautiful children, and still, I worried about my body size, about what other people thought of me, and about whether or not I was good enough. I tried so many different diets, it feels like I've tried them all! I took up running and bootcamp. I even started running half marathons. All of these physical activities were used to overcompensate for eating.

But it didn't seem to matter how far I ran; I still wasn't the "right" size. I once ran a half marathon on a treadmill on Thanksgiving morning so that I could "enjoy" dinner with my family without guilt. Another time, I ran a half marathon with a stress fracture in my hip, too worried about what I would look like if I stopped running as if there's someone I'll disappoint by admitting that I'm injured. I kept this up into my thirties, silently punishing myself for the DNA my body was born with. I got up with the sun to push myself to the brink of exhaustion and to make sure I was everything for everyone. I ran a full marathon for my fortieth birthday, convinced that if I could just achieve the next goal, I would be free of all the shame. And yet, I wasn't.

On a hiking trip with friends, I suffered a traumatic event that led me to seek counseling. I thought the incident was all I needed to talk about with my counselor, but boy was I wrong—and thankfully so. She listened to my words but heard the story beneath what I was saying. She listened hard enough that she heard the shame I had been carrying around all these years. When I finished what I thought was my story, she pushed for more. She found that place of sorrow inside me and opened it wide up. She taught me how to listen to my own body to actually hear what I was feeling. She taught me that my thoughts are just that—thoughts; they do not necessarily equate to reality. She taught me about diet culture and the lies society tells us. She taught me about my own worth.

I started changing the information I took in and actively sorted the misinformation from the truth. I did the scary things; I opened up about my insecurities to my husband and about my weight and body issues to my friends and family. I stopped pushing myself to run when it hurt. I ate chocolate when I felt like it. I accepted the changes my body was experiencing and, little by little, I grew into myself. I learned to forgive myself, to let go of my shame, to embrace who I was. I learned that just being myself is the best version of me. I accepted that there is absolutely nobody to perform for because there's nothing that I need to prove. It was hard, and it was scary, but the things I worried about most did not happen. My husband loves me no matter what size I am and regardless of how many emotions I have. My friends still want to be my friends, even when I show them my true self and don't join them on all the runs. It turns out the opinions of everyone else just don't matter.

Sometimes, I still have moments of self-doubt when society's diet culture and "feminine" expectations creep in, and I have to take back ownership over my story. There are so many days when I just feel lighter because I don't waste all my thoughts obsessing about food and exercise and the *what-ifs*. I don't listen to a never-ending cycle in my head about what I should or shouldn't have said, or what I should or shouldn't have done. What I know now is that learning to love yourself is the absolute best gift you can give yourself because it will make your life better, fuller, brighter. And that is how we win.

This may be my own personal story, but I'm sure it resonates with a lot of women out there. Sometimes, I think about who I used to be and how a lot of women are possibly still struggling through the same thing, and my heart breaks. That is why I decided to write this book.

In this book, we'll dig deeper into the challenges that we as women face in society and how we can overcome them through some practical exercises, as well as what's called the "7 Dimensions self-care framework," which consists of self-love, self-confidence, self-consciousness, self-history, self-compassion, self-talk, and self-joy.

It took me decades and one traumatic experience to rewire how I viewed and treated myself, but I'm grateful for the journey, as it will now allow me to share with you all that I've learned. I hope that your self-love journey doesn't take as long as mine did. I hope that you can start loving yourself and living your most authentic life sooner.

Your presence, thoughts, and body matter. It's time to take up space; are you ready to begin?

What is Self-Love?

I CELEBRATE myself and sing myself,
  And what I assume you shall assume,
For every atom belonging to me as good belongs to you.
I loafe and invite my soul,
I lean and loafe at my ease observing a spear of summer grass.
—Walt Whitman

What you just read was an excerpt from a poem titled "Song of Myself," written by the American poet, essayist, and journalist, Walt Whitman. In the poem, Whitman spoke of being a perfectly healthy 37-year-old who was simply being in the moment, reflecting and enjoying simple things such as observing summer grass. A part of the poem talks about Whitman getting intoxicated by civilization and other people—he equates this to a house full of perfume—ultimately deciding that he should not give in and that he should stay true to himself. "I will go to the bank by the wood and become undisguised and naked," he writes. In the latter sections of the poem, he proclaims that he doesn't worry about society's trivialities as other intelligent people do. Instead, he focuses on his soul, living in harmony with other human beings, and continuing to enjoy his physical experiences. In the end, he seems fulfilled by this as he writes, "I am satisfied—I see, dance, laugh, sing." Now, if that's not someone who loves himself, I don't know what is! If only we could all be as enlightened as Walt.

The Concept of Self-Love

We see the term everywhere: Self-love. But what exactly is it, and what does loving yourself entail? Its official definition in the Merriam-Webster dictionary (n.d.-i) is "an appreciation of one's own worth or virtue," and a "proper regard for and attention to one's own happiness or well-being." Notice that it has both the words *appreciation* and *attention* which are the exact components of the concept. Striving for self-love, therefore, is striving to appreciate yourself fully—warts and all—while also attending to your needs. It requires not just a change in how you perceive yourself, but also taking consistent actions to support your physical, psychological, and spiritual growth.

It is uncertain where exactly the concept first started, but we know that it has been around since ancient Greece. The Greeks referred to self-love as *philautia* and considered it as one of the six types of love, along with *eros* (sexual passion), *philia* (deep friendship), *ludus* (playful love), *agape* (love for everyone), and *pragma* (long-standing love). Self-love is believed to have entered popular culture around the 1950s Beat Generation and the 1960s Hippie Era (National Today, n.d.).

The Benefits of Loving Yourself

Relationships with other people can, sometimes, be difficult. A good relationship requires a ton of patience, understanding, and listening. The same thing is true when it comes to establishing a good relationship with yourself. You might have already heard the saying, "You can't pour from an empty cup." That cup is you, and you hold within your vessel a finite amount of energy. The content of your cup decreases each time you spend your energy, and it is your job to ensure that you spend your limited supply wisely. At the same time, you also have to make sure that the cup doesn't consistently dry up and that there is energy left for *you*. After all, you also need energy to engage in activities that make you happy, whether that's your loved ones, your job, or your hobbies. Some things, like engaging in toxic relationships, can radically deplete your cup, and that leads to serious physical, mental, and emotional burnout which can take a long time to recover from.

Practicing self-love can help ensure that your cup never goes empty, and this results in a lot of mental and physical benefits. In an interview with Forbes Health, Dr. Elizabeth Jarquin, a licensed marriage and family therapist and wellness coach, explains that loving ourselves and taking care of our well-being is associated with decreased symptoms of stress, anxiety, and depression. With those negative emotions out of the way, our levels of happiness, acceptance, awareness, compassion, and self-esteem tend to increase. Research also suggests that when we are in a healthy mental state, our ability to empathize becomes stronger and we become less emotionally reactive to life's stressors. Because of that, our relationship with ourselves and with others also tends to significantly improve (Solis Moreira, 2023).

In another interview for Ness Labs, Eric Fields, and Gina R. Kuperberg, researchers from the Department of Psychology at Tufts University, shared that viewing oneself positively is a key component of a healthy mind and that aside from the already mentioned benefits, evidence showed that self-love also increased determination and motivation, as well as improved sleep (Asghar, n.d.).

On top of the psychological benefits, self-love pushes us to prioritize taking care of our body in the form of movement. Consistent physical activity leads to more physical benefits such as improved brain and muscle health, a calmer heart rate, a stronger immune system, and a reduced risk of developing lifelong diseases. So, yes, learning to love ourselves doesn't just make us happier overall; it also helps us live healthier, longer lives.

How to Practice Self-Love

Because every one of us has our own unique needs and we all have different ways of taking care of ourselves, self-love can look different per individual. For example, some people might regard having self-discipline as the highest form of self-love. While for others, it might be allowing themselves to rest and recover. If you don't know what self-love looks like for you yet, don't worry, that's completely normal! Life experiences are vital to shaping who we are and helping us become more attuned to our inner selves. In the meantime, try a little bit of everything and see what fits and feels right to you! Below are some ideas you can try.

Stop comparing yourself to others. As social animals, comparing ourselves to others became a natural part of our evolution. Its purpose is to assess our place within a group so we can determine how strong our position is or how well we are performing—something that our ancestors definitely found necessary to survive in a tribe. Nowadays, that tribe seems bigger and wider than ever. We don't just have the ability to compare ourselves to people we see every day, like our neighbors or coworkers, or friends. We also now have the ability to compare ourselves to complete strangers—all you need is a smartphone and an internet connection, and you've got the recipe for jealousy and self-doubt at your fingertips! If you are guilty of this, I want you to stop scrolling and put your phone down. Before telling yourself the ways in which you are not enough and how you should be more than who you are right now, I want you to imagine that you're telling those words to your younger self. You wouldn't be that cruel to a child, would you?

Don't worry about other people's opinions. How many times have you stopped yourself from doing something you really want for fear of looking stupid? Maybe it's dancing outside in the rain or asking the waiter for more sugar for your coffee. Maybe it's keeping your apartment pristine even though no one is there to see it but you, yet the fear of someone potentially seeing it and judging you is enough to scare you. Other people's opinions can also affect you in more impactful ways, like taking a flashy job you hate, staying in an unfulfilling relationship, or compromising your core values. I have news for you. Something you probably already know deep down; you just need to be reminded more often. It's this: You can't be perfect for everybody. You can't please everybody, and you can't live life never disappointing anyone. It's simply impossible. When you feel the urge to put up a perfect facade to save yourself the wrath of other people's disdain, remember that other people are too self-absorbed to be thinking about you. Even if they do think negatively about you, that is not within your control and, therefore, not your problem. Think about all the genuine connections you could lose by pretending to be everyone but yourself.

Allow yourself to make mistakes. Doesn't it feel like the older we get, the more pressure there is to never fail, to never allow a toe to step out of line? This is especially true once we've cultivated this perfect persona in front of other people that we are someone who can do everything and do it well, someone who rarely needs help, who is the go-to person when everyone else is stuck in a bind, and the woman who always seems to have her life together? But as the old saying goes, nobody is perfect. These pressures that we rarely place upon other people and yet expect from ourselves all come from one thing: Fear—of being judged, of not meeting some standard, of not being good enough as you are. Try to constantly assure yourself that, first and foremost, you ARE inherently enough and will always be. Then, assess your choices by asking yourself, "Am I doing this because I truly want to or because I'm scared of not meeting a standard set by society or other people?" Start making choices based on the former and see how that makes you feel.

Remember that your value doesn't lie in how your body looks. Listen, I get it. It's extremely difficult to remove our sense of value from our physical appearance. We have this perception that society celebrates and treats attractive people better. This is constantly and subliminally imposed upon us through pop culture, media, and print—hello, women's magazine covers—and even in daily conversation, with the terms "pretty privilege" and "the halo effect" becoming common knowledge. This worldview is so damaging that up to 46% of female college students in South Korea have undergone plastic surgery, with most of them citing that "attractiveness was a crucial factor in seeking employment" as a major reason (Jin & Whittall, 2022). However, Kjerstin Gruys, an assistant professor of sociology at the University of Nevada, Reno—and author of "Mirror,

Mirror, OFF the Wall: How I Learned to Love My Body By Not Looking at It for a Year"—begs to differ. Reviewing multiple research projects surrounding the topic, Gruys concluded that differences in life experiences, when reviewed closely, were actually statistically insignificant. She suggests that even if a person were able to improve their appearance, they would have to change from being "exceptionally unattractive" to "strikingly beautiful" in order to experience any meaningful benefits, which is simply impossible, even with modern-day technology's help (Gruys, 2019). If that is the case—that our looks insignificantly affect our success and worth as a person—wouldn't it be freeing to let go and simply be you? So, wear what makes you feel good, style your hair the way you want to, and present yourself in a way that feels authentic to who you are. It will help you feel happier and more confident, which is a success in and of itself.

Don't be afraid to let go of toxic people. This one is something that takes time and experience to learn. When we were children, our environments were not something we could simply get out of. Whether that's being born in a toxic household, having a toxic family member, or being around bullies in school, we couldn't easily remove ourselves from the situation and so we learned to adjust and adapt. Understandably, we could sometimes unconsciously bring these feelings of being stuck and helpless into adulthood. So, assess your relationships. Does spending time with this person make you feel good or bad, light or heavy, happy or upset? Relationships, of course, aren't always butterflies and rainbows, but it also shouldn't be so hard that your physical and mental well-being is consistently compromised. If it is, then it might be time you remove yourself from the presence of that person or limit the access they have to you. It's not disrespectful and it doesn't make you a bad person.

Process your fear. As previously mentioned, a lot of what's keeping us from fully embracing who we are is driven by fear. Whenever we participate in activities that promote self-love, we have to be mindful of our intentions and ensure that we are doing them so that we can face our fears and not simply make ourselves busy and block them all out. I know someone who, in desperation, asked their therapist if they are inherently broken because they feel like nothing was working even though they were doing the things that were supposed to make them happy. They were moving their body, eating healthy, going outside for a walk daily, socializing, and engaging in their hobbies. Their therapist urged them to look within and advised them that, sometimes, even healthy activities can be used as distractions to avoid facing difficult emotions. Until our negative emotions—like fear—are faced, it would be difficult to make true progress. Remember, self-love not only involves actions, but it requires reprogramming of our minds as well. Journal about how you're feeling and what you are currently afraid of or reach out to a trusted friend or a professional to help you feel safer in processing your feelings.

Trust yourself to make good decisions for yourself. Every relationship needs to have trust at its foundation. The same is true with your relationship with yourself. This can be difficult if, in the past, you've been constantly doubted and put down. If you always hear others say that you are "a mess", "a failure" or "you can't do it," your inner voice—you know, that voice in your head that is constantly offering its loud opinions—might echo the same sentiment. Similar to the earlier suggested activity, when you are beginning to doubt yourself, imagine yourself as a child. You wouldn't want to put her down, would you? Instead, you would want to cheer her on and encourage her to keep going. Tell her she's brave and that she can do whatever she puts her mind to. Remember that you are the one who knows yourself best. You are constantly figuring out what's good for you with every setback and success you experience. So, be your best advocate and trust that when faced with a decision, you would know what to do because only you know what's best for you.

Take every opportunity life presents or create your own. Life is never going to be as perfect as we want it to be. Sometimes, this leads to us deciding to choose options that we are not truly happy with or that cause us to compromise who we are. We think that "when the timing is right," or "when we are ready," we would make a change and go for what we truly want. However, timings rarely align with our plans. So, even when things aren't perfect, don't hold yourself back from taking or creating amazing opportunities for yourself. The more you place yourself in line with what you want, the more likely it'll cross your path. In order to win the lottery, you have to first buy a ticket, right? The same is true with your goals and dreams. You have to put your name in the hat. Don't self-reject; pave your own way instead.

Put yourself first. Flight safety briefings always remind you to "put your oxygen mask on first before you help others." That's because, as we now know, you can't really pour from an empty cup. It may sometimes be difficult because nobody likes disappointing anyone. However, when faced with a choice between choosing yourself versus disappointing somebody, choose yourself. The other person might react negatively, but the right people—those who are worth spending time and energy with—will understand your boundaries. It's not being difficult or selfish, it's simply valuing and respecting yourself. Besides, you will find that you are more effective at helping other people when you are showing up as your best self, but you can't do that if you're always putting yourself last. Think of yourself as your best friend, the most important person in your life, the one who you'll always pick up the phone for no matter what time they call, and make her the top priority...because she should be. You should be.

Feel pain and joy as fully as you can. Every feeling serves a purpose. Our feelings tell us something about ourselves, even the negative ones—even pain. When we are faced with pain, it makes us want to run for the hills and never come back. It's the worst feeling! However, the reason we react to it like that is not because of pain itself, but because we tend to attach self-judgment to it. When we are in pain, negative rumination immediately rears its ugly head, telling us how awful and miserable we are as human beings. Pain then, in our minds, equates to failure, ugliness, weakness, shame, guilt, and all the awful things, but it doesn't have to be this way! Try to consider that pain might be telling us something positive about ourselves too. Pain can mean that we cared deeply about something, that we are trying, that we know our worth, so it hurts when other people don't treat us the way we deserve to be treated, that we loved, that we experienced happiness, that we are simply human. If you could think of it this way, it might make it easier for you to sit with the hurt and to really feel it fully without having to put yourself down in the process. That is the first step towards true healing. On the other side of the coin, there's joy. You might be thinking, "Why would anyone have difficulty with joy?" but it could actually be a challenging emotion to embrace for some people. We are always on the go and focused on either the future or the past. Because of that, the present moment tends to pass us by. Similar to pain, the moment something lights up your heart, try to stop and take a moment to just really feel it. Think of it as if you just climbed a mountain. After all, you went through to get to the top, wouldn't you want to stay and appreciate the view longer? You wouldn't be in such a hurry to leave, would you? Also, the more you practice being fully present, the more observant you become, and you'll find that more of life's simple joys will present themselves freely to you eventually. So, whenever you feel afraid of "getting in your feels," always remember that joy and pain are universal experiences and that means you are never truly alone.

Exercise boldness in public. This one can be especially difficult if you consider yourself a "people pleaser" because your first instinct in any situation would be to not rock the boat and to ensure everyone is happy—even if it means biting your tongue a lot. You probably have a hard time saying 'no,' sending your food back or disagreeing with someone else's opinion. You find it almost impossible to express yourself when you feel slighted or uncomfortable, and yet, you are always the first one to apologize. Some people might confuse these behaviors as simply wanting to be kind, while for others it's more complicated and can stem from their childhood or even their culture. If you keep dismissing your thoughts and feelings for the sake of others, however, you eventually "erase yourself." This means that you are actually holding yourself back from living an authentic life and creating genuine connections. Eventually, you might start viewing your relationships as burdens and you might feel constantly drained because your side of the relationship was never present to begin with. So, take small steps to exercise boldness in public. Say 'no' to invitations, speak up when you're given the wrong order, respectfully disagree and voice your own opinion, and be your own advocate. Remember that even kind people are allowed to have boundaries—they actually should! So, be kind to others as much as you can, but be kind to yourself all of the time.

See the beauty in the simple things. It's important to have dreams and goals, to imagine what your life should be like in six months, a year, or five years. This helps us focus our attention on the work required to get there. However, as you fix your eyes on what's ahead and in front of you—like your work laptop or your craft—don't forget to pause and look at what's around you as well. Using the same analogy we used earlier about climbing mountains, remember to enjoy the journey. You might get too caught up in wanting to reach the top or with how you're feeling at the moment that you fail to notice the beautiful landscape surrounding you. There's beauty in the small, simple moments—in the soft changing of seasons, in the quiet coffee break within a hectic day, in the conversations that make us laugh, in the flowers blooming as spring arrives—and it would be a shame to not notice them. So, take a brief pause, look around often, appreciate the beauty that is ever present around you, and practice gratitude as often as you can. These are essential in helping you find more joy and meaning in your life. It also makes the day-to-day more memorable!

Be kind to yourself. I cannot stress this enough: Be your best advocate—even against your own mind! It takes time to change the way you talk and think about yourself, especially if the voice in your head has always been a mean inner critic. However, you have to remember that your thoughts don't necessarily reflect reality. And that harsh voice that keeps putting you down? She's also not truly you! When you find your inner critic talking cruelly to the person in the mirror, try to treat it as a friend. When our friends are upset, we often ask clarifying questions to get to why they are upset in the first place. You can do the same towards your inner critic. Ask her what made her so upset and then follow it up with a lot of why questions. You will learn that, at the root of it all, it's often because of fear. Confront that fear with facts. Is there real-life evidence to support your fears? Asking yourself questions not only helps you get to know yourself and your emotional triggers better, but it also helps sort out facts from anxieties. Kindly explain to your inner critic why she's wrong and why you're actually going to be alright. Or simply acknowledge how she's feeling and comfort her, just as you would do for your upset friend. It definitely takes time and effort, but the more you do it, the easier it becomes to treat yourself more kindly. Soon enough, your kind thoughts will manifest themselves into actions, and you'll be able to better sort out which decisions you are making out of fear versus out of self-love.

Become more mindful. So far, we've discussed the importance of being mindful of your feelings and your surroundings, but it's also important that you are mindful of yourself. That means really digging deep and getting to know what makes you who you are, who you want to become, what your wants or needs or motivations are, and what you need to celebrate or improve within yourself. It's difficult to take care of something if you don't know how to effectively do so, and that includes you. Understanding oneself is essential to self-love.

Take actions based on needs rather than wants. When someone doesn't have a good understanding of themselves, "follow your heart" may actually not be the best advice. The heart is fickle; it changes when you do. It yearns for what's familiar and comforting, but the things that bring up these feelings in you might not necessarily be good for you. It is actually quite common for us as humans to engage in destructive behaviors in an attempt to self-soothe, but the comfort never lasts, and it might even lead to feelings of shame and regret. So, think of the person you want to become and visualize your most favorite self. What do you need to do to be her? Is it to cut back your alcohol intake, or maybe add more physical movement to your life, reduce your working hours, or maybe seek a therapist? Once you figure out your needs, say 'no' to anything that doesn't align with them.

Practice good self-care. When we accept ourselves with kindness, caring for ourselves becomes easier. Even if you don't particularly feel like taking care of yourself, do it anyway. Taking action, even when you don't feel like doing so, can help influence how you feel. For example, there's research that shows that even fake smiling can make people feel happier (Coles et al., 2019). While you can't avoid doing the inner work forever, taking care of yourself externally in the meantime can still help you progress in your self-love journey. Remember to nourish yourself daily by catering to your most basic needs. Get enough sleep, practice good hygiene, eat foods that give you more energy and make you feel good, stay hydrated, move your body, interact with your loved ones, and so on. Again, if it helps, you can think of yourself as a child. You wouldn't simply watch on as they neglect themselves, would you? You'd take care of them during the times when they can't. So, do the same for you. You deserve to receive care, and who better to give you that than the person who knows you best? You!

Make room for healthy habits. Adding to the above point, strive to include self-care activities within your daily schedule. Engaging in healthy activities consistently will turn them into habits and once that happens, it'll require less effort from your end to get yourself to do them. For example, if you want to build the habit of walking outside for 30 minutes every day, you'll probably feel the strongest self-resistance during the first few days. About a month in, however, it will be almost like second nature to you because by then, it's just a part of your usual day. The more healthy habits we build, the better we feel about ourselves.

It is important to note that the way you practice self-love can change over time. What you need when you're 21 years old may not be the same when you get to your 30s or 40s or 50s, and that's okay! There is no strict "self-love formula," and what works for you might not work for others. The important thing to know is that it is a consistent practice. Your life, circumstances, and needs may change, but as long as you continue to work on loving yourself, you are doing great!

The Myths Surrounding Self-Love

In an ideal world, everyone would have fully understood by now the concept of self-love, especially since the term has made its way into popular culture. You see it almost everywhere now, mostly to sell products where women are the target buyers, such as makeup, jewelry, clothes, shoes, bags, and so on. And while taking care of yourself can look like a shopping spree to you once in a while—*which there's nothing wrong with as long as it adds value to your life and it isn't done in a way that's unhealthy*—using *self-love* as a sales buzzword does, unfortunately, promote a shallow understanding of the concept. Corporations will try to convince you that if you love yourself, you deserve to buy their products. However, it is almost never mentioned how self-love involves a lot of inner work and even lifestyle changes. Because of this, there are a lot of myths and misconceptions surrounding self-love. Let's explore and debunk some of them.

Myth #1: Self-love is selfishness. Unfortunately, being labeled 'selfish' at least once is probably inevitable as you go through your self-love journey. This will usually come from people who have not done the necessary inner work themselves, which is why they might view your boundaries or opposing perspectives as a personal attack. Selfishness is taking action with only one's own interests in mind, completely without considering other people. In situations where there is no way to compromise in a way that makes everyone happy, weighing the scenario at hand and choosing the option that best gives you peace is not the same as being selfish. It may seem like a thin line, but no one should ever make you feel bad for prioritizing your well-being. As previously mentioned, how can you pour from an empty cup? To make others happy, you first have to be happy, and that is in no way selfish.

Myth #2: Material beauty equals self-love. As previously mentioned, self-love involves a lot of self-reflection and inner work. While taking care of yourself is a part of that, it isn't the same as surface-level self-care. Haircuts, mani-pedis, or keeping up with the latest fashion trend is all well and good; however, you can't determine someone's relationship with themselves based on that. Alternatively, if you have what society deems as an ugly style or natural nails, that doesn't mean you don't love yourself. Someone can present themselves to be the most fabulous woman in the room yet still hate themselves.

We have to be really careful with turning self-love into a competition against each other, or into another shallow standard we're supposed to be meeting to validate our own worth. True self-love looks past the material world and doesn't pressure you into fitting certain criteria to be accepted by society. Self-love encourages you to be confident and unabashedly you.

Myth #3: Self-love is egotistical and self-centered. Excessive conceit, arrogance, and narcissism are traits that are not aligned with self-love at all. People who truly love themselves don't have to act like that because they don't have anything to prove to anyone. When you truly love yourself, you easily extend that love to others. You learn how to respect and accept people as they are because you know that each person is worthy of kindness just like you are. You've shown yourself love and compassion, so you know how to show that to others too.

Myth #4: Self-love is for the weak. When you judge yourself for being weak as if that's something you're not allowed to be, where do you think that comes from? Never admitting to weakness or asking for help is another symptom of perfectionism, which as we now know stems from fear. It's your inner critic telling you that if you let your guard down and admit to softness, other people will judge you and not love or accept you. However, no one is solely weak or strong. All of us are both. Each of us has our strengths and weaknesses that make up who we are. No matter what those are, everyone needs to learn how to love themselves. Doing so will actually make you stronger in ways that actually matter. When your sense of worth and happiness comes from within yourself, you will no longer be afraid that others won't love or accept you. And that's a superpower that can never be taken away from you!

Action Steps Towards Self-Love

Earlier, we briefly touched up on some of what you can do to start your self-love journey. However, I did promise you specific and practical advice, and I plan to honor that promise! Remember that you don't have to do all of these. Try out a few and see what best works for you.

Keep a Gratitude Journal

As you are already aware, practicing gratitude only opens you up to more things to be grateful for. What better way to remember the day than documenting positive moments? That's where a gratitude journal comes in! Start it with, "Today I am grateful for..." and fill in the blanks. If you need more inspiration there are many options for gratitude journals out there to get you started. Journaling is not only a great way to honor the day but to also reflect and identify opportunities in which you could be kinder to yourself. So, you don't have to limit yourself to writing only about what you're grateful for; you can also let off some steam by writing about what might have triggered a negative response in you and why, or you can even write an encouraging letter to past/present/future self if you'd like. It's really all up to you! Remember, no one has to read your gratitude journal unless you want them to. This is something that you do for *yourself,* so YOU make the rules.

Give Yourself Compliments

Another good way to slowly change the way you speak to yourself if you are working on your mean inner critic is to compliment yourself often. You don't have to be perfect before you allow yourself to do this, because no one is. It can be something as simple as, "My hair looks healthy and shiny today," or "I have kind eyes." If you don't feel comfortable talking to yourself, it might be best to set aside time in the day for this activity. You can do it in the morning in front of a mirror while you're getting ready, or you can write it down in your journal before going to bed. The more you compliment yourself, the more you are training your mind to see the good you already possess. If you're having a bad self-love day and you really can't bring yourself to think of anything nice to say about yourself, try encouraging words instead. Positive affirmations, such as,

"I can get through this," and "I am worthy of love and kindness," are great for when you need that extra love.

Speak to Yourself as You Would With a Friend

I know I keep telling you to imagine yourself as your best friend, and you might be wondering why. Well, that's because we often set impossible standards for ourselves that we don't set for people. For example, you would never constantly point out your friend's "flaws," dismiss their feelings, or discourage them, right? And usually, even though you might not always agree with your friend, you are still able to accept them fully as they are. You even like them because they are exactly who they are! But we often don't extend that love, kindness, and acceptance toward ourselves. We can truly be our own worst enemies sometimes! So, whenever you speak to yourself, try to imagine that you're saying the words to your friend. Is it something you would say to them?

Practice Mindfulness

As previously discussed, being mindful is an essential part of the self-love journey. However, I understand that it's easier said than done. No worries, as I said before, this takes time and effort—that's why the verb "practice" is used! It's a lifelong thing, and you will only keep getting better and better at it. So, what are some things you can do to train yourself to become more mindful? Well, for one, journaling is already a great idea because it helps you pause, look within, and reflect.

Meditation is also a great idea because it requires you to stay still and focus your attention solely on your thoughts, breathing, and feelings. A misconception about meditation is that you're supposed to "clear your mind," hence, have zero thoughts. A lot of people give up the first few times when they realize that they just *can't stop thinking* and conclude they must be doing it wrong. That's not the case! Clearing your mind means that you focus on your current thought, acknowledge it, contemplate it, then let go. Then, after a while, another thought pops up and you repeat the steps over again.

Meditation is something that is supposed to help you connect with yourself and with the world around you, so there's no perfect way of doing it. Also, if you feel like you're too busy to squeeze it into your daily schedule, remember that there's no rule as to when and how long you're supposed to meditate. Only got five minutes for it? No problem! Also, nowadays, there are tons of meditation apps available to help guide you so that you can do it wherever you please. It's super convenient!

Another thing you can try is to keep your screen time in check. With all of the information and media instantly accessible at our fingertips, it's easy to feel constantly overwhelmed. Your job might already be requiring you to be in front of your computer from 9 am to 5 pm, add to that the fact that a lot of our communication nowadays is done via messaging apps, and that's already a big chunk of the day looking at a screen! Not to mention social media, online shopping, Netflix, YouTube, and so on and so forth—it's a recipe for burnout! And it's not just you. Research has shown that high amounts of screen time *does* affect our mental health and are associated with having a negative self-concept (Williams, 2022).

Don't get me wrong; technology is awesome and an extremely useful tool when used correctly. However, like with everything else, it's best to exercise moderation. You don't have to swear off smartphones, laptops, and TV altogether, but you can definitely decide how much time and energy you spend on them. Check your phone's settings to see how much time you spend on each app. Do you maybe unconsciously spend three hours a day on Instagram? You don't have to go cold turkey and uninstall it completely—*unless you want to and feel like that's what's best for you, of course*—but you can maybe decide to reduce that by an hour or so. Try to replace staring at your screen while scrolling with another activity you enjoy. It can be a hobby that you always put off doing because you can never find the time to do it or a new craft that you're trying to learn. Make small changes one at a time, divert your time and energy to something screen-free, and see how that makes you feel.

Another free and easy way you can practice mindfulness is by simply spending time in nature. Go on a hike, take a stroll at a park, or even just chill in your garden. Spending time outdoors is good for your mind, body, and spirit. It has been proven to reduce anxiety, increase energy, and help with sleep. Some people even use a therapeutic technique called "earthing" or "grounding" wherein they place their bodies in direct contact with the Earth. This can be done by walking barefoot, lying on the ground, or swimming. This is in the belief that the Earth's surface possesses a limitless supply of free or mobile electrons, which has a positive effect on our bodies. More research needs to be done about earthing, but scientific studies so far have shown that it does come with mental and physical health benefits (Locket, 2019).

If you are more of an active person, you might enjoy activities such as yoga, stretching, walks, and so on. Simply moving our bodies help us become more mindful because when we move, we become more aware of our bodies' sensations.

You don't have to limit yourself to these suggestions, of course, but I hope you get the idea; and as you can see, it's not meant to be complicated and time-consuming at all!

Celebrate the Small Wins

Having big goals is great, but sometimes we beat ourselves up for not attaining those goals as quickly as we'd like. As you know by now, the journey is just as important—if not more. So, set milestones and celebrate when you meet them. Remind yourself that you are doing a good job and growing as you go. Winning doesn't even have to pertain to life goals; it can also be winning in your day-to-day life. Were you able to spend time with nature today? That's a win! Did you have a good time with a friend you haven't seen in a long time? Another win! Finished a chore? You're a winner! The more we do this, the better we are at identifying our strengths and the simple joys of daily life.

Focusing on your own progress also means you are less focused on what other people are doing and, therefore, less drawn to compare yourself to them. So, remember that nothing you do is too small—celebrate yourself and celebrate it often!

Limit Time on Social Media

There is no denying that social media has now become a staple in a lot of people's lives. And by a lot, I mean approximately 3.4 billion people were online in 2019 alone (Ortiz-Ospina, 2019). However, it is also an established fact that social media can negatively impact one's mental health and can even aggravate underlying psychological conditions. Research has shown that "social media envy" can cause anxiety and depression symptoms, and healthcare professionals are urged to consider a person's social media use when coming up with treatments (Karim et al., 2020). Even knowing these risks though, we still can't seem to disengage from our social media apps completely. We do it for different reasons: Fear of missing out (FOMO), to control our self-image, for entertainment, or for escapism. And it's not entirely your fault if you are finding it difficult to close the apps because they are specifically designed that way—addicting and unputdownable. However, it doesn't mean that we can't do something about it. As always, the key is to moderate your engagement with it. Some tips to tame your social media use are: Uninstall at least one app and keep only your favorites, use apps designed to "lock" after a limit has been reached, utilize your phone's Do Not Disturb mode to silence notifications or put your phone in another room where you can't easily access it.

Find Support if You Need It

When you are not used to asking for help, admitting that you need support from other people might prove to be a challenge. As previously mentioned, however, self-love doesn't happen overnight. Asking for support is another thing you can practice! Find an area or task that you are having trouble with and share it with your most trusted loved ones. Allow them to listen and offer insight. If it makes you more comfortable to open up to a stranger, opt for a professional like a therapist. The more you practice seeking support from other people, the more your fears of not being perfect will be silenced as you'll continue to realize that most people, especially those who love you, are actually more than happy to support you. Opening up to them might even strengthen your bond with them.

Create a Personalized Self-Love Plan

If you like arts and crafts, are into vision boards, or if you are into making calendars and to-do lists, you might enjoy creating a self-love plan. It's basically like any other plan wherein you can write down your goals, the steps you plan to take to achieve them, your motivations, and even timeframes—again there are no rules here, do you! You can use physical materials, or you can make it online; be as creative as you can be! Remember though that the purpose of a self-love plan is to have something tangible that you can look at to remind, inspire, and motivate yourself to continue your self-love journey. Embrace flexibility within this plan and release unrealistic expectations from it.

· ♥ · ♥ · ♥ · ♥ · ♥ ·

Self-Love Story You Need To Learn From Today

As the only mixed-race kid in class, Naomi has always felt different. Her skin, hair, and body shape even looked different from the rest of the kids in school. However, being different started to equate to being less when other people started judging her negatively. In an article for the HuffPost UK (Hinde, 2017), Naomi shared that even as an adult, she is still not free from disrespect, especially on social media. She would get rude comments about her weight and looks all of the time.

Naomi shares, "I'm half Jamaican, and I was raised the Rasta way. We're really open about our bodies. Anyone with any type of figure will rock crop tops and short shorts, and no one will look at you funny. They don't care about that. It's about being happy. It's just freedom."

So, what does she do with all the negativity? She has learned not to let it get the better of her. She says that she loves how she looks, and she continues to wear her clothes and move her body in ways that make her feel good. "When I go out, I put on an outfit that shows my shape, and I stand out; people notice me. They say I look nice."

Naomi's advice? She says, "It feels good to feel good in your skin."

Chapter Activity: Create Your Own Self-Love Journal!

Now that you have learned all about the concept, components, and benefits of self-love, here's a fun activity to try where you can apply all your learnings from this chapter: Creating your own self-love journal! To get you started, here are some journaling prompts you can use:

List at least three things that you admire about yourself. Elaborate on your choices.

What are you grateful for today?

Is there anything you'd like to forgive yourself for?

What compliments have you received recently? Which ones are your favorite and how did hearing them make you feel?

Are you going through something challenging at the moment? How do you think it is making you grow?

What is your favorite unique trait of yours and why?

What are you most proud of about yourself?

What activities make you feel good, and how can you do more of them?

What is your favorite and least favorite part of today?

Write a letter to yourself as if you are talking to your best friend. What would that look like?

You can make your self-love journal the old-fashioned way and use a notebook, or you can do it on your phone or computer. As always, YOU make the rules!

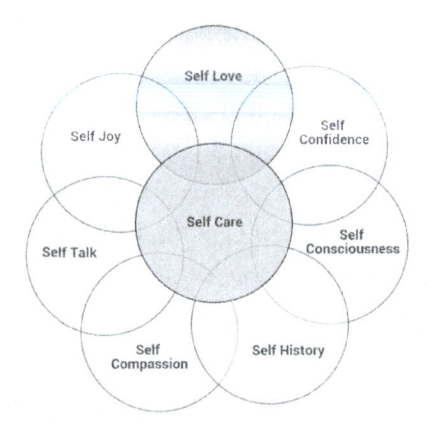

- Self Love
- Self Joy
- Self Confidence
- Self Talk
- Self Care
- Self Consciousness
- Self Compassion
- Self History

Boosting Your Self-Confidence

*T**he moment you doubt whether you can fly, you cease forever to be able to do it.*

—J. M. Barrie

According to the Women's Confidence Report published in 2021, only 3.4% out of the 11,176 global participants reported feeling highly confident. When asked to rate their confidence level from one to 10, with one being extremely low and 10 being high, most of the participants—24.4%—rated their confidence level a six, which still falls under the 'low' umbrella (IT Cosmetics & Eranos, 2021). A study (Exley & Kessler, 2019) also showed that close to 80% of women struggle with low self-esteem and self-promotion in the workplace. The study observed that "women subjectively describe their ability and performance to potential employers less favorably than equally performing men." In other words, due to a lack of confidence and self-advocacy, four in five women may be held back from advancing in their careers.

What these all tell us is that most women around the world do not feel confident at all, and it's costing us. This is sad news, but it is also totally unsurprising. I get it; we all do. It's time we change that, one confident woman at a time.

Reasons for Women's Low Self-Confidence

You might be wondering why men never seem to have this problem, or at least not as common as women do. The research I mentioned earlier supports this. It has found that although men and women had the same average scores on tests, women rated their performance poorer compared to the men, but why is that? Why do we not seem to give ourselves enough credit?

The Negative Bias of the Female Brain

A study conducted at Harvard Medical School comparing male and female brains could give some explanation. According to the study, women have larger volume in the frontal and limbic cortices. The former is mostly involved in higher cognitive functions, which includes language learning, judgment, impulse control, and conscientiousness. The latter, on the other hand, is responsible for emotion regulation. Since these parts of our brain are larger in volume, researchers believe that this may be why women are better at collaboration, empathy, intuition, and self-control. On the flipside, it also means we tend to worry and ruminate more often than men do, and that we are more prone to automatic negative thoughts (ANTs) directed at ourselves, which can eventually tear down our self-esteem (Goldstein et al., 2001).

On top of that, there's research showing that men produce more serotonin by at least 52% compared to women. Serotonin is a chemical in our brain that helps us feel calm and is involved in a lot of basic human functions such as mood, sleep, pain, and appetite. Our brain's anterior cingulate cortex also appears to be more active as observed via brain imaging scans. All of these combined make us more prone to getting stuck in negative thinking or behaviors, as well as having a more pessimistic view of the world and of ourselves (Nishizawa et al., 1997).

Other Factors That Affect Confidence

Biology is not the only contributing factor to low self-confidence. There are psychological and environmental factors that are also at play here. When dealing with confidence issues, it is often difficult to pinpoint just one root cause. Often, it's a combination of multiple factors, such as a person's environment or their physical and mental well-being.

Environmental factors can include having an unhappy childhood, having critical parents or teachers growing up, poor academic performance, stressful life events, or being in unhealthy relationships. Psychological factors, on the other hand, include mental health illnesses or disorders. Lastly, physiological factors such as living with a chronic or serious illness, a physical deformity, or a disability, also need to be considered.

The Concept of Self-Confidence

Now that you have an idea as to why women are more prone to having confidence issues, let's talk about what we can do about it. Let's first start by understanding what *self-confidence* actually is.

Self-confidence is closely related, but not identical, to two other concepts: *Self-esteem* and *self-efficacy*. Self-esteem is all about your feelings about yourself, while self-efficacy emphasizes the degree to which you believe you can do something. Self-confidence, on the other hand, requires a little bit of both! It focuses on the acceptance of your whole self, as well as how you act because of it. One definition of self-confidence states that it is "a positive feeling about oneself and the world that leads to courageous actions born out of a sense of self-respect" (Peterson, 2022).

To help us better understand, here are a few examples that illustrate what self-confidence looks like. Self-confidence is:

- Knowing that you are imperfect but feeling good about yourself anyway

- Knowing that you are worthy of respect and kindness from

other people

- Knowing that you have strengths and weaknesses, and accepting that they are a part of who you are

- Valuing yourself no matter what

- Having the courage to stand up for yourself and take up space

Therefore, self-confidence doesn't mean that you view yourself as perfect, or think that you should be. It doesn't come with unrealistic expectations, standards, or a problem-free life. Most of all, once again, it's not about being selfish.

The Importance of Self-Confidence

You've probably experienced refraining from applying for a job, or auditioning for a part, or entering a competition, even when you are aware that your skills and abilities meet—*and sometimes even exceed*—the requirements for it. This scenario perfectly demonstrates how a lack of self-confidence can negatively affect the quality of our lives. See, it doesn't only affect us internally, it also influences the lives we create for ourselves and what that looks like. Having low self-confidence makes us doubt ourselves and our abilities. It makes us feel unworthy or inferior to others. It leads to apathy, joylessness, and, sometimes, even mental health challenges, such as anxiety and depression.

On the other hand, having self-confidence makes you aware of your strengths and limitations, which allows you to create a life with space for both. It allows you to accept your faults and past mistakes, and makes you realize that perfectionism is both impossible and undesirable. It leads to inner peace, the feeling of completeness, the ability to create and experience happiness, and the ability to love your whole self even when you don't like some things about yourself.

Again, it doesn't mean you don't have to work on improving your weaknesses; it just means that you don't beat yourself up in the process, and that you know that your flaws or mistakes don't make you less deserving of kindness and respect—from both yourself and other people.

How to Develop Self-Confidence

In Chapter 1, you learned that there are some things you can do to practice self-love. Similarly, there are things you can do to develop your self-confidence. So, if you feel like you're not your most confident self at the moment, don't give up just yet and read on!

Reassess Your Locus of Control

The phrase 'locus of control' was coined in 1954 by an American psychologist named Julian Rotter. The word 'locus' is synonymous with location, so you can look at it as the place where your sense of control lies—which can be *internal* or *external.*

People with an internal locus of control look within themselves when assessing life situations. They believe that their own abilities, hard work, attributes, and decisions determine their success. Regardless of whether things go their way or not, they focus on *their part.* On the other hand, people with an external locus of control look out to the world to make sense of situations. They tend to believe that luck, fate, and circumstances determine their success. Regardless of the outcome, they focus on the external components surrounding what happened. Locus of control, therefore, refers to our perception about the underlying main causes of the events in our lives. While it's wise to have a full grasp of any situation, people with an internal locus of control do tend to be more self-confident, according to research (Heinström, 2010).

To boost your confidence, it is, therefore, important to focus on the positives of any experience, both your own and those you observe in others. Working on constantly reframing your negative thoughts can help you achieve this. For example, when you find yourself thinking, "What I did wasn't impressive because a lot of people can also do it!"

Counter it with, "What I did was impressive, and I made use of my skills to achieve that. That means I am good at what I do."

Another common negative thought that we have is, "It's all my fault that I didn't get the job!" Try to assess what you could have done better and what factors are out of your control. Afterwards, reframe your thoughts to, "I could have done better in the interview; however, the interviewer and other candidates' performances could have also influenced the outcome, and those factors are out of my control."

Step Out of Your Comfort Zone

Think of your comfort zone as your bed; just as you like it and, obviously, super cozy. You love it; you can do all the things you enjoy while you're on it. You can scroll through your phone, read a book, or binge-watch a TV series. It doesn't expect or require anything from you. Ah! Isn't that such a relaxing image? However, no matter how much we enjoy lounging in our beds, we can never really stay there forever. Wanting to do so will only lead to a number of problems and will keep us from growing, thriving, and gaining new experiences.

In the Merriam-Webster dictionary (n.d.-a), the official definition of 'comfort zone' is, "The level at which one functions with ease and familiarity." It is a mental state we reach that does not allow for personal growth to happen. Although it may seem nice at first, after a while, it becomes less stimulating. When we do the same things over and over, we tend to shift to autopilot and rely more on muscle memory. This makes our minds and spirits less engaged, which ultimately might make us feel empty. Leaving your comfort zone can help boost your confidence because it allows you to set new goals and take steps to achieve them. The more you challenge yourself, the more you overcome. And the more you overcome, your belief in yourself and your abilities get stronger.

Identify Your Strengths and Weaknesses

As previously discussed, self-confidence requires acceptance of both your strengths and weaknesses. What are you good at? What are you not good at? You probably already have an idea as to how to answer these questions. Still, it could be helpful to list them down. Similar to how you make a pros and cons list, simply create two columns—one for strengths and one for weaknesses. Then, you can use the following questions to help evaluate yourself:

- What have others complimented about me?

- Which occasions/situations did I require the help of others?

- Which activities make me feel drained?

- Which activities have I spent hours doing without seemingly feeling tired?

- What are my favorite hobbies and why?

After answering these questions, it's time to get the input of people you trust. I know…it can seem mortifying at first! However, it's actually extremely helpful. That's because, as you already know, when we struggle with self-confidence, we tend to be more critical of ourselves. Ask your closest friends or significant other what they think your strengths and weaknesses are. Also, remember that each one of us has our own biases, and we each see the world through different lenses, so try to simply listen and accurately take notes. Do not make excuses for any perceived weaknesses or dismiss any of their compliments. This will help you get more accurate data.

Work on Your Self-Talk and Self-Care

In Chapter 1, in learning to love ourselves better, you learned about the importance of positive self-talk and practicing good self-care. Similarly, these two are also important in developing self-confidence. When you talk to yourself as if you are talking to a friend, you are more likely to believe in yourself and cheer yourself on. You are more open to taking risks and charging headfirst towards new opportunities. You will also be able to accept your shortcomings with more grace and kindness for yourself. All of that helps boost your confidence.

How we care for ourselves is important too. Do you ever notice how confident you seem to feel immediately after getting your hair or nails done? Or whenever your clothes make you feel and look good? Even simple things such as brushing our teeth, getting a full night's rest, washing our hair, eating healthy and satisfying foods, and hydrating ourselves throughout the day give us that confidence boost too! The more we take care of ourselves, the more we feel like our favorite selves, and the more we, therefore, like ourselves.

Action Steps Towards Developing Self-Confidence

Now that you have a better understanding of self-confidence, it's time for some easy, practical tips that you can incorporate in your day-to-day life. Whenever you think you need a quick confidence boost, try out some of these suggestions.

Shift Your Posture

Whenever you see someone who appears confident, try to observe their posture. As we learned in the previous chapter, our actions can influence how we feel. In a 2012 study, Harvard psychologist Amy Cuddy tested participants by giving them a mock job interview. Prior to the "interview," participants were asked to adopt different poses: High-power poses, or low-power poses.

High-power poses are open, relaxed, and allow you to fully expand your chest and lungs, making you breathe more deeply. Hands-on-hips, standing with a wide stance, or raising your arms in a V-shape, are some examples of it. Low-power poses, on the other hand, are the complete opposite. It is where the body is closed and guarded. Sitting with your arms crossed over your chest, hunching, and "hugging" yourself by having one arm across your body are just some examples. The results of the experiment showed that those who adopted high-power poses prior to the evaluation performed better during the interview and presentation and were more likely to be chosen for the job (Cuddy et al., 2012). So, if you're feeling a little nervous or insecure, try changing your posture! Sit up straight or stand in a high-power pose and smile. Think of yourself as if you are regal because you are!

Wear What Makes You Feel Good

I can't count the number of times I blamed myself for not looking great in an outfit that I wanted when the truth was the clothes simply weren't in my correct size. If I had a dollar for every pair of jeans I wiggled myself into or dress zippers I forced to close, I'd have, well, lots of dollars! We could all use a little reminder sometimes that clothes are supposed to fit us, not the other way around. It is not a personal fault if we ask for a different size or for size adjustments.

On top of that, wearing clothes you don't feel comfortable in because they are trendy—or because other people like them—dims your shine! Don't be afraid to try on different styles to find out what makes you feel good. Wearing clothes you like makes you feel more yourself, and therefore, helps boost your confidence.

Transform Nervous Energy To Positive Energy

Every time we are faced with uncertainty, especially if other people's attention will be on us, it is impossible not to feel butterflies raging in our stomachs. It revs us up, makes our hearts pound, fills us with so much jittery energy that we can't stay still, and makes the room seem extremely bright and sharp. However, did you know that instead of trying to calm down, it might actually be best to keep this energy going? The trick is to reframe nervousness into excitement instead. That's because the feeling of anxiety and excitement is physiologically almost the same as both of these feelings prepare our bodies for action (Whitener, 2021). In fact, a 2014 study showed that individuals who reappraise their anxious feelings as excitement *did* feel more excited and performed better compared to those who simply tried to calm their nerves down. It's believed that the reason for this is because it prevents us from getting stuck in a "threat mindset," and instead, shifts our brains into an "opportunity mindset" where we see every obstacle or uncertainty—like a job interview, a speech, a stage performance—as an opportunity to learn and grow (Brooks, 2014). So, the next time you feel a surge of nervous energy, try saying this out loud to yourself: "I am excited!"

Move Your Body Regularly

As previously mentioned, self-care is an extremely important factor in developing self-confidence, and part of that is engaging in physical activities daily. Don't you simply feel happier and more productive after even just a short walk? It's an established fact that moving our bodies immediately enhances our mood and makes us feel more positive. It also makes us appreciate our body's abilities and physique more, as well as provides us with a sense of accomplishment. These consistent positive feelings directed towards our bodies *do* help with our self-perception, and therefore, our self-confidence.

Visualize

Have you ever heard the phrase: *The power of visualization?* It's a useful technique wherein you "picture" what you want to happen in your head, instead of what you don't want to happen. For example, whenever you think, "I'll come off as awkward, insecure, and weird," visualize that you'll come off as confident and charismatic instead. Picture the scene and do a play-by-play: How is the confident 'you' entering the room, standing, speaking, and socializing? What does she look like as she does these things?

Seeing yourself succeed, even if it's all in your mind, helps you believe that you can make it happen. When you "practice success," you are able to study each step you need to make towards it, which you can then replicate in real life. A study even proves that imagining the movements you want to make—or what's called *mental training*—trains your physical muscles almost as much as actually moving them does (Ranganathan et al., 2004). Also, have you ever noticed that asking your brain not to do something only reinforces the idea in your mind? Simon Sinek, an American author, shared the best example for this: Don't think of an elephant! Now, what are you thinking about? Don't make the elephant pink; don't make it wear a hat! Again, what are you thinking about?

Telling our brains to focus on 'not messing up' only makes us fixate on the ways we could mess up more. Instead, it will be more helpful to shift our focus as to what could go right and how we could succeed (Winner Spirit, 2022). I'm a big fan of visualization because there truly is power to it. A lot of athletes, actors, CEOs, and politicians also swear by it. As Muhammad Ali once said, "If my mind can conceive it and my heart can believe it, then I can achieve it."

Allow Yourself To Make Mistakes, Take Risks, and Trust the Process

Whenever we're evolving and stepping out of our comfort zones, mistakes are bound to happen. There will also be moments when we will be required to take risks. However, instead of panicking, approach these changes as opportunities for growth—because they are! When you get into the "opportunity mindset," as we have discussed, you will become more accepting of your mistakes, which helps develop self-confidence because you gain new knowledge and wisdom after every trial and error. Similarly, when we take risks, we are given the opportunity to see ourselves in a whole new situation. Hence, we are reminded of how able and resilient we can be, which influences how we view ourselves. Again, developing self-confidence takes time and consistent practice. There will be moments when you will feel like you're wandering in the mist, but there's a lot to be learned while you're there.

Take it one step at a time and trust the process. The mist will blow off eventually.

Clarify Your Goals

There's nothing more empowering than making progress towards personal, meaningful goals. That feeling of accomplishment is where self-confidence grows. Therefore, it is only reasonable that we clarify what our actual goals are. Doing so not only allows us to focus our energy into a specific direction, but it can also help weed out what goals we have that are genuinely ours and what we took on for the sake of other people. For example, we may be striving towards a specific job title, even though we don't actually care about the title or the job, and we're simply aiming for that goal to impress other people.

When deciding on a goal, think **S.M.A.R.T!** This acronym stands for **S**pecific, **M**easurable, **A**ttainable, **R**elevant, and Time-bound. The S.M.A.R.T approach has been proven to help set clear and realistic goals and is incredibly popular in the field of self-improvement and habit formation. For a detailed how-to guide, head on over to the end-of-chapter activity!

Other Self-Confidence Action Steps

Some of the steps you can take to develop self-confidence, you actually already know! Mindfulness, speaking to yourself as a friend, and asking for help when you need it, do not only help with self-love, as discussed in chapter one, but self-confidence as well.

·♥·♥·♥·♥·♥·

Self-Confidence Story You Need To Learn From Today

Content creator Hamel Patel opened up to Cosmopolitan India (2020) about her self-confidence journey. She shared that, growing up, people have always commented on seemingly *everything* about her. Because of that, she developed a lot of insecurities, which took her years to get over. When she started being more open about this topic on her social media accounts, she felt a strong sense of community start to form.

"While sharing my experiences helped my followers embrace themselves, it also showed me that I wasn't alone in how I felt," she said, "Being vulnerable and sharing my insecurities with my community on Instagram has helped me overcome them to an extent."

She notes that there are still some days when her insecurities get the better of her. During those days, she says she gives herself a little extra love. Overall, however, she has grown more confident, mostly seeing her body as—in her own words— "a powerhouse," but she wants to remind everyone that this didn't happen overnight.

"Undoing what society has instilled in our brains, was a process, and it didn't happen overnight," Hamal said. "I was constantly telling myself that I didn't have to look or act a certain way to be considered 'beautiful' because all of us were made unique, and that's what 'beauty' truly is."

Chapter Activity: Set Your Own S.M.A.R.T Goals!

As discussed in this chapter, S.M.A.R.T stands for **S**pecific, **M**easurable, **A**ttainable, **R**elevant, and **T**ime-bound. For this activity, you are going to set a S.M.A.R.T goal by answering some questions. Again, you can do this the old-school way by using pen and paper, or you can do this on your phone or laptop. Format and design it as you please. As always, do YOU!

1. **Specific.** Depending on what's most applicable, you can change *specific* with the words *simple, sensible,* or *significant*. In setting a specific goal, asking yourself the five "W" questions is a good starting point. Try to answer each one:

What is it that I want to accomplish?

Why is this goal important to me?

Who will be involved or affected by this goal aside from me?

Is there a specific location needed to achieve this goal? If so, where is that?

Which resources or lack thereof do I need to keep in mind?

1. **Measurable.** You can replace *measurable* with the words *motivating* or *meaningful*. The aim is to identify how you can keep track of your progress as you go along the journey. Tracking your progress not only helps keep you motivated, but it also gives you an idea of how to overcome any challenge that comes your way. Ask yourself the following questions to get started:

For how long will I work on this goal?

How many milestones are there within this goal?

How much money/time is needed from me to achieve this goal?

What does success look like?

1. **Attainable.** You can also use the word *achievable*. While working towards a goal definitely comes with challenges, it is important that whatever goal you set, it is not impossible to achieve. Here are some questions you can ask yourself to check if your goal is within the realm of possibility:

Assessing my overall situation, is this goal realistic?

From where I am right now, how can I make sure I accomplish this goal?

1. **Relevant.** Other words you can use are *reasonable, realistic,* or *results-based*. It seems similar to the previous step, but this time, assess whether your goal aligns with who you are, your long-term goals, and your short-term goals. If your answer to these questions is "yes," then your goal is relevant:

Does this align with the person I want to become?

Is this goal worthwhile?

Is this something I want for myself?

Can this be achieved alongside my other goals?

Is this the right time to start working on this goal?

1. **Time-bound.** The purpose of this step is so that you can set up milestones to focus on as you work on the bigger picture. Once you reach a milestone, you can assess whether you'd like to create a different goal altogether or continue with the current one. Think of it as a regular check-in to assess whether the goal still stands or if it needs to be tweaked to accommodate life's constant changes. Try answering the following questions to get started:

When do I expect to accomplish this goal?
What does a month from now look like?
What progress should I expect to have made six months from now?
What can I do today to make progress towards this goal?

Now that you've set a **S.M.A.R.T** goal, place your work somewhere easily visible or accessible so that you can be reminded every day of what you are working towards. Remember; the journey is just as important as the destination, so don't forget to enjoy the ride!

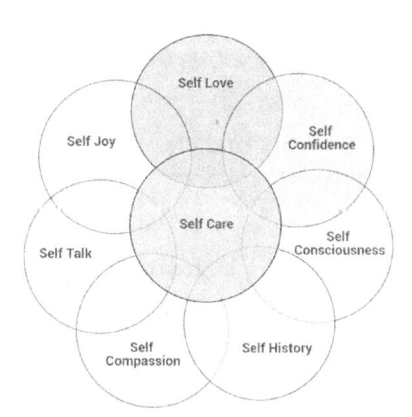

Giving Your Body The Positivity It Needs

One day I decided that I was beautiful, and so I carried out my life as if I was a beautiful girl. I wear colors that I really like, I wear makeup that makes me feel pretty, and it really helps. It doesn't have anything to do with how the world perceives you. What matters is what you see. -Gabourey Sidibe

Body positivity has become such a hot topic in the media in the last few years that it has divided people. If you really think about it, isn't that strange? To be debating women's bodies, how we should look, and how we as women should feel about the way we look. The way female bodies are represented in the media still leans heavily towards an "ideal" that is able-bodied, slim, toned, and perpetually young. It's no wonder that body dissatisfaction is prevalent, with approximately 91% of women resorting to diet culture to achieve an ideal body shape, when the truth is that only about 5% of women naturally possess the body type often portrayed by the media (Runfola et al., 2012). However, that rarely stops us from seeking it for ourselves. Unfortunately, when doing so, we don't take nutrition and our overall health into account, which makes us prone to developing an unhealthy relationship with food. The fasting, constant dieting, binging, or purging that women do for an ideal body is what leads to the development of eating disorders, which can happen unintentionally (Do Something Org, n.d.).

On top of this, a 2011 survey conducted by Glamour magazine involving 300 participants of all sizes found that a staggering 97% admitted to having an "I hate my body" moment in a day. The same survey found that, on average, young women have 13 brutal thoughts about their bodies in just one day (Dreisbach, 2011). Also, 95% of those struggling with eating disorders are between the ages 12 and 25 (Cambridge Eating Disorder Center, n.d.). Women everywhere, especially young ones, are suffering, and we should be concerned.

What Is Body Positivity?

There's a lot of misinformation surrounding body positivity nowadays, but before we get into all that, let's discuss what body positivity actually is.

We can trace its roots in the late 1960s where the "fat acceptance movement" was born, which rejected society's fat-shaming culture and weight discrimination. Born from this movement was The National Association to Advance Fat Acceptance which was established in 1969 with the goal of changing how we, as a society, view and talk about our weight.

In 1996, a psychotherapist who had experienced having an eating disorder, founded a website called "thebodypositive.org." The site's aim is to offer resources and materials designed to educate people on how to focus away from losing weight and into feeling good about their bodies instead. This is where the term "body positive" first emerged. It later became a worldwide movement with the help of Instagram hashtags—such as #BodyPositive and #bodypositivity—in 2012 as many users posted photos of their unedited bodies as a way of body acceptance and celebration (Huntington, n.d.).

Body positivity is "the assertion that all people deserve to have a positive body image, regardless of how society and popular culture view ideal shape, size, and appearance" (Cherry, 2020). It has two elements. The first is the acceptance of all bodies regardless of their shape, size, and features. The second is a focus on health and functionality over appearance. Its ultimate goal is to promote body inclusivity and diversity, meaning the acceptance and celebration of all bodies and the appreciation of our bodies' differences. It's important to note that the body positivity movement is different from the body neutrality movement, which instead focuses on our body's function and, therefore, doesn't put much importance on celebrating or loving its appearance (West, 2022). People who are recovering from eating disorders, or those who feel like loving their bodies is an impossible task, may find that body neutrality works better for them instead.

Here are some examples of what body positivity looks like:

- Appreciation of unique aspects of your body

- Gratefulness for your body and its functions

- Admiration for your body's features regardless of whether or not they meet societal ideals

- Feeling comfortable and confident in your own skin

- Focusing more on what you like about your body instead of what you perceive as your 'flaws' or 'imperfections'

- Rejecting the negative messaging and information about bodies

Reasons for Needing Body Positivity

A negative body image has been shown to increase the risk of engaging in unhealthy lifestyles or behaviors. This includes dieting, drastic weight control behaviors, and restrictive or disordered eating. Dieting is the most common symptom of having a negative body image, and it can seem so innocent and trivial in the beginning. For example, someone who just wants to lose a few pounds for an upcoming event may start dieting on their own—or with the help of millions of non-medical sources out there claiming you can "*lose weight fast*"—without knowing that dieting poses a significant risk for developing an eating disorder. Even 'moderate' dieting has been shown to increase this risk because, while dieting has been normalized in our society, it is not naturally normal or healthy for our bodies (Better Health Channel, 2023). A negative body image can lead to a wide range of health conditions such as mood disorders, body dysmorphic disorder, eating disorders, muscle dysmorphia, relationship problems, and self-harm tendencies. People with anxiety, obsessive-compulsive disorder, or depression are also more prone to having a negative body image and are, therefore, more prone to fall victim to dieting (Stanborough, 2020).

On the other hand, research suggests that body positivity has significant benefits to our health and overall well-being. Having a more positive body image has been shown to lessen depression symptoms, improve self-esteem, decrease unhealthy dieting behaviors, and increase protective intentions toward one's body (Gillen, 2015).

Myth: Body Positivity Supports 'Obesity'

As I mentioned at the beginning of this chapter, there is a lot of misinformation surrounding body positivity. The most prevalent and persistent is this: *Body positivity supports obesity*. First, let's align our understanding of the term 'obesity.' To do that, we must discuss the body mass index or BMI. You probably already know BMI as the most commonly used predictor of health. Its calculation is based on the ratio of someone's height and weight. But how accurate is it really?

The problem with BMI is that it is an oversimplified equation focused on appearance, not overall health; the history surrounding the establishment of BMI even supports this statement! BMI was first created in the 1830s by a Belgian statistician, sociologist, astronomer, and mathematician Lambert Adolphe Jacques Quetelet, who was interested then in finding "*l'homme moyen*," or "the average man." It is important to highlight that Quetelet was not a medical professional and that his intentions were never to look into 'obesity' or health. Furthermore, the participants in his experiment were mostly Western European men.

Then, in the 1970s, a Minnesota physiologist named Ancel Keys wanted to have an easier way for insurance companies to estimate people's body fat because, at the time, insurance companies were simply making guesses. Like Quetelet, the participants in his experiments were mostly healthy, middle-aged men. He concluded that Quetelet's BMI was the solution, and thus, BMI made its way from insurers into the clinical realm (Truu, 2022). In 1998, the National Institutes of Health changed the BMI 'overweight' threshold from 27.8 to 25, making 29 million Americans—*who were considered 'normal' weight prior to this*—'overweight' overnight. Critics noted that taking part in drafting these guidelines was the International Obesity Task Force, which was principally funded by two companies selling weight loss drugs (Butler, 2014).

As you can see, BMI's origins and history are dicey at best. It also tells us that there were a lot of factors that weren't considered when developing BMI, such as women's naturally changing bodies, age, race, and ethnicity. More recent research proves the reliance on BMI to be archaic and problematic. For example, a 2013 analysis conducted by the National Center for Health Statistics, covering over 3 million people and 97 studies, showed that while the World Health Organization (WHO) considers a BMI of 25-29.99 'overweight,' it is actually the healthiest weight for middle-aged Americans (Flegal et al., 2013). Athletes are also a good example, as they often have higher BMI than what is considered standard, yet most of them are healthy (Callahan, 2021). That's because BMI can't tell the difference between body fat and muscle weight, and thus, it isn't a great indicator of an individual's health. Also, a 2016 study that measured other health indicators such as blood pressure, cholesterol, and insulin resistance, showed that 29% of those considered 'obese' were metabolically healthy, while 30% of 'normal' weight individuals were cardio-metabolically unhealthy. The study urged policymakers to consider the "unintended consequences of relying solely on BMI" (Tomiyama et al., 2016).

Body positivity, on the other hand, does not focus on the numbers on the scale. It focuses on rejecting the negative biases surrounding weight. Labeling people as 'overweight' or 'obese' based on their BMI opens them up to the stigma surrounding those labels and, therefore, makes them more prone to negative biases and harm. For example, society has this misconception that a person is 'obese' not because of underlying physical or mental health factors, but because of sheer laziness. You probably hear this message every day—in gym advertisements, vitamins or supplements commercials, and even in toxic reality TV shows. The message is loud and clear: "If you are 'obese', it's because you are lazy, and, therefore, it's your fault and you should be ashamed," or "If you are struggling with 'obesity', just eat less and exercise more; it's not that hard!" This is exactly what body positivity is trying to fight.

Body positivity urges society to grasp the idea that everyone—no matter their weight or appearance—deserves inclusion, appreciation, respect, kindness, and representation. The body positivity movement's mission is to promote inclusivity and diversity for all.

The Importance of Self-Acceptance

Self-acceptance is an extremely important component of body positivity. Self-acceptance, according to one definition, is "an individual's acceptance of all of his/her attributes, positive or negative." According to research (Morgado et al., 2014), there are three main attitudes that make up self-acceptance: *"Body acceptance," "self-protection from negative judgments from others,"* and *"feeling and believing in one's capacities."* It allows us to properly evaluate our features and accept any perceived negative aspect as part of who we are.

A lack of self-acceptance has been known to be the main contributor to a lot of health concerns, such as the development and maintenance of eating disorders, 'obesity', having a negative body image, and mental health conditions. Aside from physical and psychological concerns, one's quality of life can also be heavily impacted; people who lack self-acceptance have been observed to have trouble socializing, have difficulty maintaining relationships, have low confidence, and show a lot of self-hatred (Gupta, 2022).

On the other hand, self-acceptance has been shown to decrease the following: Depressive symptoms, the need for other people's approval, fear of failure, and negative self-talk. Therefore, self-acceptance increases happiness, positive emotions about ourselves, a sense of freedom, self-worth, self-esteem, and independence (Virginia Department of Health, n.d.). Here are some of the reasons why self-acceptance has such a positive effect on our well-being and the quality of our lives (Woods, 2018):

Self-acceptance requires us to develop humility with ourselves and the world.

Self-acceptance helps us see things and experiences as they actually are, rather than how we would like them to be.

Self-acceptance allows us to become better problem solvers.

Self-acceptance helps us become more confident and, therefore, opens us up to having healthier relationships.

Self-acceptance helps us get to know our own selves better.

Self-acceptance allows us to forgive ourselves and others.

Self-acceptance contributes to feelings of inner peace.

Self-acceptance allows us to be more in control of our attitude and actions.

Deconstructing Diet Culture

We can't talk about positivity without also taking a deep dive into "diet culture." Diet culture is described as the "pervasive belief that appearance and body shape are more important than physical, psychological, and general well-being" (MacPherson, 2022). Nadia Craddoc, a UK-based body image researcher, explained this further by saying that diet culture is the "collective set of social expectations telling us that there's one way to be, and one way to look, and one way to eat and that we are a better person, we're a more worthy person if our bodies are a certain way" (Tagle & Schneider, 2022).

While you're probably not consciously participating in diet culture, I'm sure you are already mildly well aware of it because it is simply inescapable in our society. When someone claims they are on a diet, nobody even bats an eye; we just get it, and we sometimes even applaud them or envy them for it. It is also not uncommon for our new year's resolution lists to include "lose weight" every year. Also, if I say I'm having a "cheat day" by eating a slice of pizza, you understand what I mean immediately without me having to expound. If I declare that "salads are good, cake is bad," you might even agree with me on that statement. This focus on weight and dieting, as well as the normalization of labeling food as either good or bad—*proper or cheating*—are evidence of how prevalent diet culture is in our society.

We can also look at the numbers published by the CDC. Between 2013 to 2016, it's been recorded that approximately 49.1% of Americans have tried to lose weight within the past 12 months, 56.4% of which are women. The most common method is a combination of exercising and eating less food, also known as 'calorie restriction' (Martin et al., 2018). This happens even though there's research that shows that dieting rarely works in the long term. In fact, dieting is actually considered "a consistent predictor of future weight gain," according to a study (Wolpert, 2007). The same study stated that dieters can lose five to 10 percent of their weight initially, but the weight comes back, and as much as two-thirds of dieters regain more weight in four to five years, compared to what they initially lost. This is what's called 'weight cycling'—where you are constantly putting your body through a pattern of losing and gaining weight—and it can lead to adverse health outcomes. In conclusion, dieting is not safe and effective.

How to Deconstruct the Diet Culture

Even with what we know now, it can be difficult to rewire our brains from equating health and fitness to thinness, because it's what society has been shouting at us since birth. Along with our knowledge of the ineffectiveness of BMI and dieting, here are ways how we can bid diet culture good riddance:

Know that health and beauty standards are always changing. Remember when we collectively shut those high-waist jeans of the 80s into the fashion vault, shook our heads, and swore they would never see the light of day again? Four decades later, they're back in style, and we wonder why we ever got rid of them in the first place. The same is true with health and beauty standards; they come and go. And just as you master one trend, another one has already taken its place. Take for example the Brazilian butt lift (BBL) era of the mid-2010s which emphasized the beauty standard for women to have small waists and big butts. As a result of this trend, BBL cosmetic procedures boomed (Ardrey, 2023). Nowadays, however, #BBLEraIsOver has been trending, and there's word—*and concerns*—that "90s thinness" is making a comeback. Both trends are horrifying and show us how much we need body positivity now more than ever.

Identify and interrogate fatphobia and diet culture messaging on multiple levels. Since diet culture has managed to seep its way into almost everything, we have to become aware as to which messages, biases, and ideas are coming from fatphobia and diet culture. To do this, we must look at three different levels: *Intrapersonal, interpersonal,* and *institutional.* Let's start with ourselves and look at it at an *intrapersonal* level. To do so, think about how diet culture influences the way you feel. You can start by asking yourself questions like, "What is causing me to view my body negatively?" or "What external factors are causing me to not like my body, and how do I respond to them?" Then, look at how other people treat you because of fatphobia or diet culture messaging; this is the *interpersonal* level. Are they making judgments about your body or about what you eat? Are they persuading you to join a gym, and what are the reasons for that? Last is the *institutional* level. This can be a lot trickier, but the more you start to observe, the better you will get at discerning which messaging comes from fatphobia. Look at ways in which diet culture creates barriers for everyone. For example, do bus seats take into consideration all types of bodies? Does the company or brand you support sell products that take into account all shapes and sizes? Do people get discriminated against because of their weight, and in what ways? How does weight bias display itself in the workplace? Those are just some of the questions to ponder upon.

Make a conscious effort to be mindful of the language you use and the feedback you'll accept. Diet culture has conditioned us to take the phrase, "You lost so much weight!" as a compliment. And it's true that the intention behind it is rarely malicious; however, commenting on a person's body, as we now know, can be harmful no matter what our intentions are. We never know what someone is going through and how their health is. We don't know if the weight loss is intentional or due to stress or an illness. Also, commenting on someone's body and associating being thin with being beautiful is a way of us perpetuating diet culture messaging. This is one example of how we can exercise being mindful of our language. Instead of commenting on how someone looks, focus on something they've done. For example, say, "I love how you styled your hair!" instead. Also, calling someone "brave" for simply being proud of their body shape is something you should think twice about. If unsure, saying nothing is always another option. This goes for describing food as well. Avoid commenting on other people's food choices if you can. There is no inherently good or bad food. Yes, even a burger is not inherently bad, and your friend getting fast food does not mean they're choosing to let themselves go. This thinking is in line with diet culture messaging. On the flip side, this approach goes for how you receive other people's words towards you as well. If someone compliments you for being thin or losing weight, or if somebody jokes about you eating a salad because you are on a diet, use humor to correct or deflect. If that doesn't work, simply don't engage. Having a conversation about rejecting diet culture is all about choosing your battles and knowing when you are in a time and place to have that conversation. Let your comfort level direct how you handle the situation.

Practice intuitive eating to improve your relationship with food and promote healing. If you're someone like me who has been calorie counting or food restricting since I can remember, you might have a complicated relationship with food. Food may be tied to confusing, upsetting, or even painful emotions. Naturally, this shouldn't be the case as our bodies are actually wired to know how and what to eat. This innate knowledge only gets disrupted when we try to 'train' our bodies to survive on fad diets or 1500 calories a day—by the way, if you see any program promoting 1500 calories a day as a correct and safe way to diet, run from it as far as you can! Food is a basic human necessity, thus we cannot and should not try to avoid it. When our bodies need food, they will automatically tell us via hunger cues. That's where intuitive eating comes in. Intuitive eating is learning—or relearning—to trust that your body knows best and that it will work as it should. It means prioritizing the body's cues over external rules like portion sizes, calorie counting, etcetera. Because we are putting our full trust back into our bodies, it helps us heal our relationship with food, as well as helps us reject diet mentality or emotional eating. As previously mentioned, there is no inherently good or bad food. Also, there are a lot of proven benefits that come with intuitive eating such as decreased eating disorder behaviors, better nutrition choices, improved body satisfaction, better mood, and positive effects on cholesterol levels and blood pressure (Compton, 2018). Again, I want to stress that food is a basic human need. It should not be turned into something complex in the hopes of meeting another impossible standard. Intuitive eating may take some practice and, in some cases, even the help of a healthcare professional. However, it is another way of practicing self-love. What's a better way of showing self-love than trusting your body fully? Also, imagine being able to eat without fear and self-judgment; that makes all the effort worth it. Remember, no diet is the best diet!

Befriend your body. Similar to how we are working on befriending our inner voice, we should also work on befriending our bodies. The intention is the same; you wouldn't put down your friend, would you? You wouldn't tell them how ugly their body looks or how "fat" they are.

You wouldn't talk to them in a cruel way. Also, you are usually attentive and understanding of their needs. For example, if your friend tells you that "they're craving dessert," or "they want another serving of pasta," you wouldn't normally react harshly to that, would you? Befriending our bodies helps us appreciate them better because we really should do that more often. Think of all the things your body does for you and all the things it allows you to do—your lungs are literally keeping you alive right now, even if you don't tell them to! All your body asks is that you love it and care for it; it really is just like having a friend.

Build a community. No man is an island, and in this world where not everyone is ready to leave diet culture behind, it can get lonely when you decide to do so. However, you are definitely not alone! It may take some effort, but it helps to get in touch with like-minded people. On social media, follow accounts that promote body positivity and intuitive eating. Unfollow accounts that perpetuate diet culture or those that do not make you feel good about yourself and your values. Look for body-positive groups online or around your local area. Continue to educate yourself by listening to podcasts, reading, and having conversations. These are ways how you can find one or two like-minded people, and soon enough, you'll have yourself a community to turn to for support and camaraderie.

Understanding Societal Pressures Around Body Image

According to Thomas F. Cash, a leading expert in the field of body image, there are two views of physical appearance: The "outside view" and the "inside view." The latter is what is referred to as 'body image,' or the way we perceive how our bodies look. The former is societal standards surrounding our bodies (Cash, 1990). As we know so well by now, our *inside view* is greatly influenced by the *outside view*. It all starts in childhood when we, consciously or subconsciously, encounter societal ideals of beauty.

Although the concept of beauty is ever-changing and varies across cultures, in modern times, the Western ideal has increasingly evolved into something along the lines of both "thin" and "very fit" throughout the years. One study revealed that American women, when compared to Polish and Czech women, feel stronger pressure to conform to Western beauty ideals and have higher internalization of general body shape and an athletic ideal (Czepczor-Bernat et al., 2017). These beauty standards promoting the desirability of being unrealistically thin are spread and perpetuated through traditional media in the forms of TV commercials and magazine images, as well as through social media. One study involving college students showed that the slender ideal presented in magazines and social media was reportedly the cause of the development of their eating disorders (Kaziga et al., 2021). The same study concluded that "young people will seek to attain unrealistic body shapes and sizes largely because the societies in which they live have created these images."

A Deeper Look at the Role of Social Media

Although unrealistic beauty ideals have existed long before the conception of social media, social media now plays a major role in perpetuating them. The reason for this, as previously discussed, may simply be because social media has become such a huge part of our lives. Unfortunately, it becomes another vehicle where women are exposed to unrealistic beauty ideals, and as a consequence, feel pressure to conform to them.

Our social media profiles often provide other people with a first impression of us, and it's understandable that we want to put our best foot forward. However, with this intention of curating the best possible representation of ourselves, some people can go to extreme lengths such as editing and "touching up" images of themselves. It's extremely easy to fall prey to this line of thinking, as edited images have become so normalized. Social media comments also play a major role in heightening the pressure. Since comments are often accessible to anyone who has access to the image and comment section, it informs users as to what society finds ideal and acceptable. For example, when photos that show well-trained and slender bodies receive more positive comments and higher engagement compared to photos of bodies that do not fit the ideal standard, it subconsciously informs us of what's favorable and what's not—what we should and shouldn't aspire to be.

This can be problematic, as it is within our nature to want to be approved of and accepted by society. Human beings are social animals and, for centuries, have always lived within tribes. It is therefore ingrained in our biology to need belonging and to fear ostracization. One study showed that following appearance-focused accounts on Instagram and engaging in appearance-focused photos, such as 'selfies,' on Facebook highly correlated with the idealization of and drive for being thin (Cohen et al., 2017). However, it doesn't mean we need to ditch social media use altogether. We may just have to be more aware of our intent and actions. The same study revealed that following appearance-neutral accounts on Instagram, and general Facebook use, were not associated with the same body pressure outcomes. Therefore, the bottom line is that social media is a tool, and, like all tools, it is how we use it that determines whether we are empowered or harmed.

Shapewear and Your Level of Body Positivity

Shapewear is defined as "*underwear that fits tightly and is designed to make the body look thinner by smoothing out and holding in areas that are out of shape*" (Cambridge Dictionary, n.d.). When you think of shapewear, you might immediately think of corsets; something worn to provide the body a more 'flattering' shape—think Disney princesses with high breasts, tiny waists, and curvy sides. Basically, the exact beauty ideal that body positivity is trying to knock off the pedestal. That's why you may be wondering if shapewear is in line with body positivity, especially if you're someone who likes wearing it. Don't worry; you're not the only one asking this exact same question, it seems. It has actually been a topic either debated or avoided within—and even outside of—the body positivity community.

Still, it's an important topic, so let's talk about it. You might think that shapewear is slowly being phased out as a thing of the past, but it's actually the opposite that is true. According to a market research report, the shapewear market is expected to grow 5.8% by 2024 (ReportBuyer, 2018) and reach a revenue of $3.3 billion by 2027 (Parisi, 2022). One of the reasons cited for this predicted growth is due to shapewear's growing popularity among buyers.

Shapewear is traditionally marketed as a way to alter the body to appear thinner and more "sucked in." For example, rib-breaking corsets have been widely accepted as the norm in the past. Nowadays, even the leading brand Spanx still has a collection named "Skinny Britches." And while more recent brands, like Skims, have aimed to be more inclusive by offering a wide range of sizes, words such as "waist trainers" and "ideal silhouette" can still be seen in the language they use to market their products. Hence, the irony has been highly noted.

It is important to note that while shapewear gets a bad reputation because of how it is marketed, it has come a long way thanks to the body positivity movement. Brands are starting to include a more diverse range of product shapes and sizes and are de-emphasizing slimming. Consumers are starting to see these changes as the new standard, and companies are adapting so as to not lose customers. This is just one of the great examples of how the body positivity movement is making a change in society and making it a much better place.

Whether you want to support shapewear or not is totally up to you. As I've said, it's all about intention and being mindful. If you're using shapewear to feel good in the body that you have and not to make your body fit a different size, I fully support you! If you are mindful of the brands you support and what language they use to promote their products, you're doing great. With or without the use of shapewear, everyone should be allowed to feel good about how they look.

How To Be More Body Positive

Now that you have a better understanding of the external factors that play a major role in how we view our bodies, let's work on the internal factor: You. Aside from being more aware of diet culture and fatphobia, here are some of the things you can do to show your body the positivity it deserves:

Find things you love about your body. As you know by now, I'm a big fan of making lists! It's just such a great way of getting a visual of our thoughts and feelings. So, make a list of things you love about your body. Don't think about what other people think, what do YOU love about it? Is it the fact that your body gets you places? Or maybe the shape of your eyes? Or that mole or freckle on your face that you find interesting? List as many as you like and place that list somewhere you can see every day so that you always have a lovely reminder.

Repeat positive affirmation. Carve out some time in the day to simply be grateful for your body. Thank your body for what it does for you and tell yourself what you like about it. If it's too difficult to produce a compliment, encourage or comfort yourself instead. Repeat positive phrases like, "My body deserves to be taken care of," or "My body is a gift, and I'll treat it with love and respect." This helps because words matter and can influence our moods as well as how we view ourselves.

Stop your mind when it starts to make comparisons. Since we now know the importance of being mindful of our thoughts, the moment you catch yourself comparing how you look to others, pause and take a deep breath. Ask yourself what triggered that reaction from you, take note, and then try to avoid the trigger moving forward. For example, is it a bikini photo from Instagram perpetuating an ideal body? Does every post from that account trigger your brain into making comparisons? If yes, then there's no shame in unfollowing. Also, when you find yourself comparing yourself to other people, remind yourself that everyone, even that one seemingly perfect person, has their own flaws and struggles just like you. They may have strengths where you don't, but that means that the opposite is also true: You might have strengths where they don't. It puts everything in perspective that no one is perfect, but we are all perfectly imperfect in our own ways. Also, you can try to see behind the comparison for motivation or inspiration, instead of attaching negative feelings to it. What made you envious, and why? Is it because that person has something you are striving for? That's fine! See how you can maybe replicate what they did to achieve it. That being said, make sure you are inspired and motivated by someone who is aligned with the person you want to become—someone that can push you to be a better person—and not someone who simply makes you feel bad and not good enough.

If you can't be positive, be neutral. We touched upon body neutrality a little bit earlier, and as mentioned, being body neutral may be more effective for people who find body positivity a struggle. With body neutrality, you don't have to be best friends with your body if you don't want to, but it does require you to be cordial with it—calling a truce if you will. It's less celebration and more acceptance; acceptance that our bodies are just one part of who we are and that it was made to function in a way that keeps us alive, and that's exactly what it does. If body positivity's message is that "everybody is beautiful," body neutrality simply proclaims, "Everybody is." Focusing on the body's abilities and functions, and not placing too much importance on its appearance—whether *positive or negative*— is the core of body neutrality. In short, your body doesn't even need to enter the conversation if you don't want to. To practice being more body neutral, be grateful for all that your body does for you. For example, instead of complimenting how you look, thank your feet for getting you places, or your heart for doing its job of pumping blood. Our bodies work incessantly to keep us alive, it's important to be reminded sometimes that that's more than enough. Use body neutrality as a stepping stone on your way to body positivity.

♥ · ♥ · ♥ · ♥ · ♥

Body Positivity Story You Need To Learn From Today

In an interview for Good Housekeeping Magazine (Sutton, 2019), 50-year-old Sylvia Mac shared her story. Sylvia suffered from third and fourth-degree burns on various parts of her body after an accident involving boiling water at home. She experienced a life-and-death situation which her doctors didn't even think she'll survive. Thankfully, she did. However, she was faced with a new problem: Her burn scars. Her scars were proof that she had overcome something terrible, but all they did was cause her to feel ashamed of her body for many years. She shared that her self-esteem hit rock bottom, and it affected her mental health. She suffered from paranoia, anxiety, panic attacks, and severe depression. At her lowest points, she even had suicidal thoughts and turned to alcohol to self-medicate.

"I didn't want to be faced with a mirror. I felt ugly," Sylvia shared.

Sylvia loved swimming but she would always try to change into her swimwear after everyone else had gone, and she would dive immediately into the water so she could hide her body. After becoming a grandmother in her late 40s and realizing that her family was all looking up to her, she finally decided that enough was enough.

She was at the beach that time when she felt the courage to walk to the water's edge, pull off her body wrap, and just start waving and posing toward her mom. She said she felt like a weight had been lifted. After that moment, Sylvia started sharing her story online—something she was once too afraid to do. She also started a support group called 'Love Disfigure' with the aim of supporting people like her who may be feeling ashamed to show their disfigured or scarred bodies. Sylvia shares that for the first 47 years of her life, she felt like a victim of her own scars, but that's no longer the case now.

"In my first year, I was a survivor, and in the past two years, I've been thriving," Sylvia said.

Chapter Activity: Body Positivity Truth or Dare Game!

Now that you have extensive knowledge of how to give your body more TLC, here's a fun little game: Truth or dare! Answer body-positive questions truthfully or do a body-positive dare. You can do this by yourself or with your friends. Remember that the goal is to show your body some love and positivity—and to have fun of course!

Truth Questions:

What is one thing you love about your body?

What is your favorite body feature or part, and why?

What are your favorite ways to move your body?

What activity has your body helped you do recently?

If your body could talk right now, what would it say?

What is your favorite body pampering activity?

What food makes your body feel good after eating it?

What's the most recent compliment you received?

When do you feel most comfortable in your own skin?

What does a body positive image mean to you?

What does being kind to your body look like for you?

What would you like to thank your body for right now?

What unrealistic body expectation are you going to let go of?

What are you going to promise your body moving forward?

Dares:

Follow one body-positive account on Instagram.

Use the hashtag #BodyPositive the next time you post a photo where you felt comfortable in your own skin.

Leave one body-positive comment on someone's photo.

Write "Every Body Is Beautiful" as your Instagram bio and keep it for 48 hours.

Give the next person you see a genuine compliment.

Look in the mirror and give *yourself* one compliment.

Perform an activity that helps you move your body in a way that you enjoy (e.g., take a walk, dance, jump).

Try something new with your appearance for a week (e.g., draw on a winged eye, wear something you wouldn't usually wear, style your hair differently).

Get a piece of paper and draw a body outline, then write down everything your body does for you within it.

Throw away one piece of clothing that is in the wrong size.

Put on an impromptu fashion show for your friends.

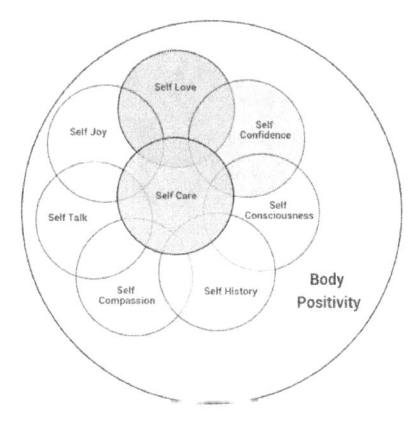

Body Positivity: Self Love, Self Joy, Self Confidence, Self Care, Self Talk, Self Consciousness, Self Compassion, Self History

A Life Without Self-Consciousness

*E**ven in social life, you will never make a good impression on other people until you stop thinking about what sort of impression you're making.* -C.S. Lewis

When Myah turned 13, one or two pimples started showing up on her face. It would go away and then come back—*and then go away and come back again*—week after week. Her friends at school started noticing and lightly making fun of it, telling Myah that her pimples "*loved her too much, they kept coming back.*" She laughed along at first, but after a while, she secretly got tired of the negative attention. This was the first time Myah felt self-conscious. Whenever she was talking with someone, she would wonder if they were noticing the red little bumps on her face. When she would recite in class, she would worry about how her face must have looked to other people. The thought made her anxious, so she stopped raising her hand altogether. Even after her friends stopped joking about her pimples, she would wonder if they secretly thought she was ugly.

One day, in the girls' bathroom, Myah was waiting for her friend Lucy, who was in front of the mirror, drawing a winged eye on her eyelids using a blue eyeliner. Myah opened up to Lucy about her dilemma, and Lucy laughed at Myah's predicament as if it was all so silly. Lucy stopped what she was doing and pulled out more makeup from her bag. She then told Myah to hold still and started working on her face. Using her makeup brush, Lucy dabbed some concealer on Myah's whole face. She then put on a liquid foundation and finished it off with loose powder. Since she was already having fun, Lucy also curled Myah's lashes and put mascara on them. "There you go," Lucy beamed, "problem solved!"

Myah was uncomfortable at first because she felt like she had too much makeup on her face. She told Lucy it felt like she had on another thick layer of skin, but when she looked in the mirror, she gasped. She reveled at how smooth and even her skin looked and how her eyes popped. Myah smiled at herself and Lucy. She was happy…and pretty!

Throughout the day, people started noticing the change in her. Her friends told her something was different about her. Girls from her classes—and even a few boys—commented on how beautiful she looked. When she got home, she opened up to her mom about wanting to buy some makeup. She insisted that since her mom and big sister were using makeup, she should be allowed to do so as well. She tried convincing her mom by saying, "I'm 13, I'm old enough," or "All my friends are wearing makeup, I'm the only one who's not!" Her mom told her that it was best if she stayed away from makeup for as long as she could and that one or two pimples were normal for a teenager. Her mom offered to take her to a dermatologist instead if she was truly worried so that they could get her skin checked. However, Myah thought a dermatologist won't be able to make her as pretty as she felt that day—with her longer lashes and her bright, perfect skin. Myah insisted, and with an exasperated sigh, her mom finally gave in and gave her the money she needed.

Myah happily headed over to the drugstore. When she got there, she was overwhelmed by the number of options to choose from, and there was no one around to help her. So, she simply tried her best to remember what Lucy used on her face; she bought items that looked similar and that she could afford with the money her mom gave her. When she got home, she perched herself in front of her bathroom mirror and immediately tried on the products. She was happy with the results. She started waking up earlier than usual so she could put on makeup before school every day.

A few weeks in, however, her pimple dilemma got worse! Instead of one or two, there were now a lot of them in varying shapes and sizes. Plus, it was everywhere on her face, and it hurt. She finally asked her mom to take her to the dermatologist. When they got there, the doctor told her she needed to learn how to properly remove makeup every day, how to clean her makeup brushes, and advised her to not put on any makeup for a few weeks to let her skin heal. The next morning, she stood in front of her bathroom mirror before school and thought about how she was the ugliest girl she had ever seen! She didn't want everyone at school to see her without her perfect skin and bright eyes. "*I don't look like myself,*" she thought, but she listened to the doctor's advice and went to school bare-faced. Still, she felt more self-conscious than ever. Even if they never mention anything, she '*just knew*' that her friends were repulsed by her skin. She stopped participating in class because she '*knew*' everyone would notice how ugly she was.

These were Myah's thoughts, but in reality, no one thought that of her. Her friends didn't know that this was how she felt, and they still saw her as the same old Myah; her classmates too were so busy preparing for finals for them to take note of how she looked. Still, the following day, Myah refused to leave the house without putting on makeup, saying she just "didn't feel like herself without it."

Just like Myah, for a lot of us, our venture into the world of makeup started when we were really young, with the intention of correcting little 'flaws' or improving a small part of how we looked. Almost immediately, makeup becomes such a part of our identity that we don't feel beautiful without it, and we end up using it consistently for the rest of our lives. One survey conducted by Nuyoo Cosmetics supports this as it revealed that about 66% of women started using makeup as teenagers, between the ages of 13 to 15. Most of them—54%—admitted that the primary reason why they started wearing makeup was because they felt self-conscious about their looks. When asked how they felt as teenagers when they went out without makeup, 34% said they felt *self-conscious*, 31% said they felt like *something was missing*, and 31% said that they felt *unattractive* (Fab UK Magazine, 2018).

There's research showing that people who are more self-conscious of themselves in public have a higher tendency to resort to fashion and makeup when presenting themselves to other people. Additionally, they tend to be more accurate in their knowledge of the impressions they leave on other people, and they strategize around this to get a more favorable response from others (Doherty & Schlenker, 1991). But what exactly is self-consciousness?

One of its official definitions in the Merriam-Webster dictionary (n.d.-g) is being "uncomfortably conscious of oneself as an object of the observation of others." Those who study self-consciousness explain that it's human nature to reflect on ourselves and how others may perceive us, and that self-consciousness can be separated into two categories: *Private self-consciousness* and *public self-consciousness*. Private self-consciousness refers to our introspective thoughts and self-reflection. This includes taking note of our own habits, thoughts, motives, and feelings. Public self-consciousness, on the other hand, is our awareness of ourselves as a social object. It's our concerns about the impressions we leave on other people, and how our behaviors, style, and appearance could be perceived by them (Davis, n.d.).

Recognizing Self-Consciousness

While a healthy amount of *public consciousness* is good, too much of it may contribute to the development of social anxiety. Healthy self-consciousness has many benefits including giving us the drive to accomplish goals, confidence, improved social skills, and a better understanding of ourselves. On the other hand, unhealthy self-consciousness can result in some problems. As we now know, a lot of people who struggle with self-esteem issues tend to view their own selves more critically. This can affect how they feel other people judge them, and they may often conclude that they are not leaving a favorable impression. Because of this, they may start to feel anxious about being seen by others, or they might develop a higher sensitivity to criticisms or rejections. This can further lead to self-isolation, which only worsens their social anxiety. Therefore, having unhealthy levels of self-conscious emotions may contribute to anxiety, depression, borderline personality disorder (BPD), and obsessive-compulsive disorder (OCD).

Self-Conscious Emotions

As mentioned, being self-conscious is simply a part of human nature! By the age of three, many children actually already have a full range of self-conscious emotions and these emotions increase as we get older. Self-consciousness develops once we start understanding ourselves, as well as societal rules and standards. That's why adolescents—who are experiencing social pressures for the first time—are more prone to higher levels of self-conscious emotions.

Now, you may be wondering what's a normal amount of self-consciousness and what's simply too much. Here are some symptoms of *healthy* self-conscious emotions (Gotter, 2017):

- Awareness of one's accomplishments and having pride in them
- Being able to engage in and enjoy social activities
- Being able to recognize one's mistakes and take ownership of them
- On the other hand, some symptoms of unhealthy self-conscious emotions include:
- Having an angry or hostile response when embarrassed
- Self-isolation or avoidance of social experiences
- Being unable to recognize one's mistakes, and placing the blame on others
- Self-blame for the wrongs made to them

- Self-esteem issues

- Feelings of agitation, nervousness, anxiety, or depression

How To Deal With Self-Conscious Emotions

If you feel like too much self-consciousness is holding you back, there are some techniques you can try. First, identify what triggers these emotions. What situations make you feel extremely self-conscious? Then, consider the possible reasons behind it. Is it simply the attention of other people, or are you worried about something specific regarding how you look?

Second, try to analyze the drawbacks that self-consciousness brings. Did feeling too self-conscious lead to you not being able to enjoy the moment? Did it lead to you not being able to participate in an activity or conversation? Also, it's important to know that one of the major issues with self-consciousness is having trouble reading and remembering situations. For example, you might have done well on a task—and the people present with you may have even told you—yet your mind can only focus on what didn't go perfectly. This can result in you questioning whether other people's remarks were genuine. Being aware of these drawbacks and tendencies can help you gauge situations more clearly and realize what too much self-consciousness is making you miss out on.

Third, practice switching to an outward focus. Self-consciousness comes from having too much focus on ourselves, so try to shift your attention to the people present with you or the situations happening around you. It might take some practice, but what you can do is try to develop a genuine interest in other people. When we are genuinely curious about something, we tend to forget ourselves. So, whenever you feel self-conscious, try to learn something new about someone else in the room. You can strike up a conversion or simply observe. The goal is not to be as confident or at ease as other people but to be more mindful of what really is happening in your surroundings. Then, compare the difference in the experience you have when you focus outwards compared to inwards.

Fourth, remind yourself that others don't typically see what you see. The good news is that other people are also so busy in their worlds that they often do not see that small wine stain on your right sleeve. If, when talking to someone, you feel worried about coming off as awkward, remember that they probably have the same worry too and that coming off as awkward or making a mistake in front of them is not the end of the world! When in doubt, ask people about themselves. People love sharing their passions and interests, so focus your attention on that. It's a great way to break the ice and shift your thoughts away from the negatives. You might even come across as a great listener or a genuine person!

Lastly, continue working on self-acceptance. We already know from previous chapters that improving our self-acceptance can do wonders to our confidence. When we are more accepting of our strengths and weaknesses, we become better at dealing with self-conscious emotions too. Also, self-acceptance allows us to let go of situations we can't control; so, if something doesn't go as planned—or if you find yourself making a mistake—you can shrug it off and learn from the experience, all the while knowing that life goes on!

Overcoming Self-Doubt Once and for All

A lot of negative self-conscious emotions are rooted in the negative ways we also view ourselves. Some level of self-criticism is perfectly normal and healthy because it helps us become better people. However, too much fear can lead to unhealthy self-conscious emotions. In order to be more confident, we have to address our self-doubt and recognize how it may be holding us back from having new experiences. So, let's talk about self-doubt. What is it exactly?

The official definitions of the word 'self-doubt' in the Merriam-Webster dictionary (n.d.-h) are "a lack of faith in oneself," and "a feeling of doubt or uncertainty about one's abilities, actions, etc."

Imagine it as a friend asking you if you are really *sure you can do this.* A little bit of concern like that is welcomed, of course, it's smart even, but when it becomes too much and too often, you always end up saying, "You're right, I can't do this." That's when it becomes a problem. There are many reasons why some people doubt themselves more than others. Most of it stems from our childhood when we were still trying to form our self-image and gathering information mostly from external factors. One example would be having narcissistic or extremely critical parents growing up. The child could grow up afraid to repeat their parents' mistakes of being too arrogant and may swing extremely in the opposite direction of being too modest or unconfident. Or the child may believe their parents' excessive criticisms and carry those within themselves through adulthood. It may be difficult for these people to accept compliments and praises and they might believe they don't deserve any positive attention.

Another potential cause of self-doubt is if a person gets so used to giving themselves "tough love" that instead of it becoming a motivator, it causes harm. These people are often afraid of being perceived as weak, "soft," or lazy. Because of this thinking, they could lead themselves to a path of self-sabotage, perfectionism, and burnout.

Past experiences can also be a potential root cause of extreme self-doubt. Past failures and mistakes really do haunt us, and it heavily influences who we are and how we view the world. Because of this, some people may view themselves as 'failures' after past setbacks and start believing it, or they may become extremely cautious and overwhelmed with self-doubt because they are afraid of experiencing 'failure'—and the negative feelings that come with it—again. On the flip side, there are also people who are afraid of success. Mostly, they simply do not want to disappoint others or appear like they do not know what they are doing. Because of this, they become afraid of making mistakes. They might harbor a fear of falling short or being unable to replicate past successes. They might also not feel deserving of their successes and believe that their achievements simply come from having great luck, and not because of their skills and talents.

If consistent self-doubt is not addressed, it can lead to a number of issues such as anxiety, depression, lack of motivation, procrastination, emotional instability, lack of self-confidence, and difficulty making decisions (Eugene Therapy, 2020).

Negative Ways of Dealing With Self-Doubt

We may never rid ourselves of some form of self-doubt but, as previously mentioned, a low level of it is not something to be worried about and is even healthy. Also, even having too much self-doubt can be managed in healthy ways, so don't lose hope! Before we jump to that, let's look at some negative ways of dealing with self-doubt so that if you recognize any of these, you can start addressing them. Negative ways of dealing with self-doubt include:

Self-handicapping. Self-handicapping, also called self-sabotage, is when we engage in behaviors that we know can jeopardize our performance or successes. Some examples are staying up late, using harmful substances, or procrastinating on a task. Someone who is self-handicapping may also choose tasks that are so easy that success is meaningless, or a task so difficult that success is unlikely. We self-handicap intentionally or unintentionally to avoid success, and therefore, also failure. It could also be used to shift or minimize blame away from one's abilities, skills, or talents. For example, if someone did poorly on a work presentation because they refused to sleep the night before, they can say that they expected that poor outcome and blame it on the lack of sleep. On the other hand, it could also be used to increase the value of one's success. Using the same example, if the presentation went well despite the lack of sleep, the person may feel better about their skills and could claim more responsibility for the success. Overall, it all boils down to the fear of being "exposed" and is intended to protect our self-image. However, it may lead to us not really being able to give a goal our best try, and therefore, can reduce our chances for success.

Overachievement. Overachievers are people who perform at a higher level and achieve more success than expected. It might sound like a desirable trait because who doesn't like more success, right? However, when we strive to overachieve in order to run from feelings of self-doubt, that's when it is harmful. Overachievers tend to prioritize achieving a goal—or a set of goals—over everything else; that includes sacrificing their own health, relationships, and happiness in order to chase a target, which is often always moving beyond them. Therefore, the problem doesn't really lie in the need to achieve, but in the means that are used to reach and maintain the achievement. Overachievers tend to tie their self-worth mostly to their achievements. For example, instead of deriving a sense of joy from being intelligent and diligent, someone might place more emphasis on having graduated valedictorian instead. Overachievers tend to celebrate the achievement, more than themselves. This need to overachieve could stem from childhood as well. If someone's parents or guardians only showed them affection after an achievement, or if the child was constantly compared to others, this could inform their worldview and they could end up believing that achievement is the only way to gain love.

Impostor syndrome. Impostor syndrome is the psychological condition of feeling like "a fraud" and having constant anxiety despite being high-performing. People who struggle with impostor syndrome often do not feel successful internally, regardless of how objectively successful they are externally. They have a gnawing feeling of self-doubt and incompetence, despite their achievements, and have a fear of being exposed as "phony" despite having legitimate expertise, education, or certifications. They often try to work longer hours and are afraid to ask questions or for help as a way of proving themselves. Because of this, people with impostor syndrome are more prone to stress, anxiety, and burnout (Paulise, 2023). A study (Huecker et al., 2023) further described it as "self-doubt of intellect, skills, or accomplishments among high-achieving individuals," and stated that there are six characteristics that may be present in someone with impostor syndrome. One is the "imposter cycle," where, in response to achievement-related tasks, the individual will either over-prepare or procrastinate. The root cause of both responses is a fear of being exposed as a fraud. After completing the task, there is a fleeting sense of success that isn't internalized and, therefore, doesn't last as the individual already prepares for the next task with the same feelings of anxiety. The second characteristic is perfectionism, which can also be expounded as an individual's 'need to be the best.' Because of this, those with impostor syndrome might be hyper-competitive and have practically unattainable self-imposed standards and goals. In relation to this is the third characteristic, called 'super-heroism,' wherein due to the individual's need to be the best, they either over-prepare or take on more work even to the detriment of their mental health. The fourth and fifth characteristics, respectively, are fear of failure (atychiphobia) and fear of success (achievemephobia). Lastly, a denial of competence and capability may also be observed. This means that people who struggle with impostor syndrome tend to discount or minimize their own intelligence, experience, skills, and natural talents. In any achievement, they would focus on what they did 'wrong' and would attribute any success to external influences like luck.

Focusing on opponents' unfair advantages. Similar to self-handicapping, one of the ways an individual could soften the blow of potential failure is by taking note and highlighting their competitors' advantages. For example, if they are being considered for a promotion at work, along with other people, they may immediately start to convince themselves that they won't get the job because someone else is closer to the boss. Doing this helps soften the blow of rejection, or if all goes well, magnify the success of the individual.

Positive Ways of Dealing With Self-Doubt

Even if you feel like you are simply built with too much self-doubt, don't give up just yet! There are healthy ways of dealing with self-doubt. Some of these things you actually already know like positive self-talk, keeping a journal, self-love, self-compassion, and mindfulness. Other ways you can positively deal with self-doubt include:

Reflect on the growth you experienced. Growth is inevitable, especially if you are practicing stepping out of your comfort zone. Even if you don't want to, something in your life that is not within your control is going to spark some growth in you. So, in times of extreme self-doubt, reflect back on these experiences, look at how far you've come, and take note of the positive ways these experiences have changed you. Remind yourself how you've made it through every tough time of your life so far and all that you've gained in the process.

Remember your achievements. As previously mentioned, people who struggle with self-doubt often fail to internalize their achievements. Now that you are aware of that tendency, you have to be more mindful of your accomplishments. Create a list of all you've achieved, big and small. Write it in your journal or snap a photo of the moment. Having concrete reminders of your achievements will help make it more difficult for your brain to deny them.

Avoid making comparisons. We know that people who struggle with self-doubt tend to focus on their opponents' advantages, so the first thing to do is to *stop looking at other people as opponents*. When you catch yourself doing so, remind yourself that you and this other person aren't in competition with each other. For example, if something about a person sparks envy inside of you, reflect as to why that could be. Use the knowledge as inspiration and transform the negative emotion into internal motivation instead.

Find validation from within. Speaking of looking internally, try to find a sense of success and contentment within too. If you can't do that yet, at least give your own self the validation that you seek. When you find yourself needing praise, attention, or validation externally, try to shift your focus within yourself. What words do you need to hear? Say it to yourself and find evidence within.

Identify your values. This one truly needs to be emphasized. When people—especially overachievers—do not take the time to identify their values, they can easily get lost in a race that doesn't even matter to them. In their need to prove that they are competent or 'the best,' they could take part in situations that will not fill their cup or give them a sense of fulfillment. It's like wandering life without a compass—without knowing which way the true north is. When you have a firm grasp of what your core values are, you can make decisions that align with them, and you won't have to spend unnecessary energy and focus on experiences that don't. Also, it will help with your self-doubt because once you weed out the paths that do not align with who you truly are, you'll be able to take more confident steps toward the paths that you do choose. It helps us know ourselves better, and as a result of that, we get a sense of clarity, peace, and trust within ourselves.

Embrace vulnerability. Due to self-doubt, we tend to keep a lot of things to ourselves. We often don't let anyone in, whether that be feelings, fears, opinions, or reactions. We fear we'll be judged or misunderstood, so we just refuse to share ourselves with other people. However, that keeps us from forming genuine connections since one of the cornerstones of friendship is being open and vulnerable with each other. A lot of life experiences also require some level of openness from us, which is why it's best to practice embracing being vulnerable instead of running away from it. In order to do so, you must first have a firm understanding of who you are, then you have to be honest about it— both with yourself and with others. Second, you must practice acceptance. Your fears may happen...or they may not! Accept that whatever the result is, you can get through it and will grow from it. Lastly, let go and break free from things and situations that hold you down. Say what you mean, let go of what didn't work out, and reach out and grab new experiences. Remember that being vulnerable makes you strong, not weak.

How To Overcome Self-Doubt

There was a lot to learn in this chapter and you may be feeling overwhelmed. You may be asking yourself, "Where do I even start?" Don't worry, I've got you! Here are some practical activities you can start doing in your day-to-day life to help you overcome self-doubt:

Meditate. Meditating—or simply engaging in activities that make us more mindful—helps because it's the opposite of self-consciousness. When you're fully present in the moment, as previously discussed, you tend to forget about yourself. Because of that, you decrease the chance of being stuck in your head, worrying about situations, and trying to control them. Listen to a guided meditation, paint, or do some breathing exercises—whatever calms your mind and grounds your body. Breathe; you got this!

Talk to yourself in the mirror. You're already familiar with this one. Carve out some time in your day to give yourself a little pep talk! It could be in the morning while you're getting ready for the day or at night before you go to sleep. Just check in and be honest with yourself. Talk to yourself like a friend and just reflect on the day. The more you know yourself, the more you trust yourself—and that's the exact opposite of self-doubt!

Go for a run. Running is another activity that helps us become more mindful, but aside from that, it comes with a lot of health benefits; improved confidence is one of them! Running has been proven to reduce anxiety, improve our mood, help us sleep better, and lower our blood pressure. It's also an activity where we feel a sense of accomplishment after doing it, which helps boost our self-esteem. You don't need to go fast and you don't need to go far - in fact, even just five minutes at a moderate pace will do the trick. (Weingus, 2017).

Cold showers to stop negative thoughts. Okay, hear me out. I know you may be raising your eyebrows on this one, but I'll just lay out the benefits of a cold shower. Aside from helping you wake up quicker and reducing muscle aches and pains, cold showers are believed to help decrease anxiety symptoms. Studies have proven that cold showers can lower your heart rate and boost your immune system too (Cherney, 2020). It may take some getting used to, but a quick two to three-minute shower will definitely help stop negative thinking.

Snap a rubber band on your wrist every time you doubt yourself. This is another mindfulness technique to literally snap you out of your spiral and back into reality. Wear a rubber band around your wrist, and every time you catch your mind starting to doubt yourself, snap the rubber band against your skin. You don't have to snap it in a way that results in too much pain, just enough to stop yourself from engaging in the thought. Then, you can start reflecting or redirecting your thoughts to something else.

·♥··♥··♥··♥·♥·

Overcoming Self-Doubt Story You Need To Learn From Today

In her post for her website, leadership and development coach Dr. Audrey Reille shared a story inspired by the common challenges her clients face. A client named Irene sought out her help because she has always struggled with asserting herself at work, and now that she was working from home, it had gotten much more difficult for her. She was worried about upcoming layoffs as well. Irene shared:

"I find it difficult to speak up on Zoom calls, and I think I am losing visibility and influence. We have a few people on our leadership team who dominate conversations and it's hard to find a good time to speak. I like to take time to think about my ideas before sharing them. So, I hesitate, time passes, we get to the end of the Zoom call, then I kick myself for not saying anything."

Irene shared that prior to working from home, she did better at meetings because everyone could see her body language and the people in the room made more of an effort to be inclusive, but even then, she recalled that she always hesitated to talk, doubting that her comments had any value.

After sharing a few more stories, it became clear to Dr. Reille that Irene was raised to be selfless and modest. Like many, she had been taught to be kind and appreciate others, but not how to do that to herself. Because of this, her personal life and career were limited by self-doubt. Irene couldn't see the value she brought to the table; hence, she couldn't show it to others. Her self-criticism and toxic self-consciousness were stopping her from advocating for herself.

Dr. Reille's advice to everyone, ask yourself what self-appreciation means to you. It doesn't even have to be self-love; just self-appreciation is enough for now. What are you good at? What do you bring to your workplace or relationships? She said that appreciating ourselves is not bragging, nor is it arrogance or vanity.

Dr. Reille reminds everyone: "Acknowledging your worth won't turn you into an egomaniac! It will make you a more effective leader and a happier person" (Reille, 2020).

Chapter Activity: 'How Self-Conscious Are You?' Self-Assessment

This assessment will help you gauge your level of private and public self-consciousness, which we learned about in this chapter. Simply ask yourself the following questions and rate yourself from one to 10, with one being '*strongly disagree*' and 10 being '*strongly agree*.' Encircle your answer, then tally up the scores at the end; the higher your score is, the more self-conscious you are. You can also take a look at how you rated each question to get an idea of what you need to start working on. Ready to start?

Private self-consciousness:

I reflect on myself constantly:

1 2 3 4 5 6 7 8 9 10

I constantly examine my motives:

1 2 3 4 5 6 7 8 9 10

I look deep into the meaning behind everything:

1 2 3 4 5 6 7 8 9 10

I examine myself objectively:

1 2 3 4 5 6 7 8 9 10

I spend a lot of time reflecting on past situations:

1 2 3 4 5 6 7 8 9 10

I tend to get lost in my thoughts:
1 2 3 4 5 6 7 8 9 10
Public self-consciousness:
Thinking about what people think of me worries me:
1 2 3 4 5 6 7 8 9 10
I want other people to see me as something special:
1 2 3 4 5 6 7 8 9 10
I easily feel threatened:
1 2 3 4 5 6 7 8 9 10
I need constant reassurance:
1 2 3 4 5 6 7 8 9 10
I seek approval from others:
1 2 3 4 5 6 7 8 9 10
I find that other people easily intimidate me:
1 2 3 4 5 6 7 8 9 10

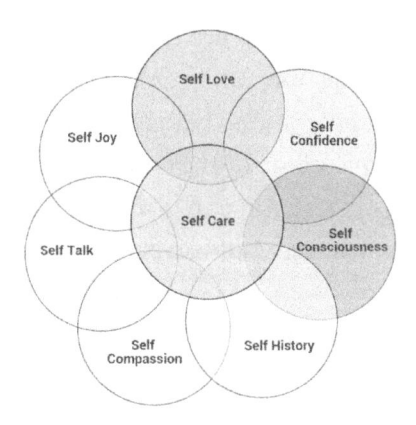

Accepting Your Own History

There are wounds that never show on the body that are deeper and more hurtful than anything that bleeds. -Laurell K. Hamilton

We've briefly touched upon how the way we were raised by our parents or caregivers can affect our self-esteem. In this chapter, we'll dig deeper into that. We'll talk about childhood trauma and how we can slowly heal or accept it as a part of our history. As we grow older and become more reflective, we slowly realize how impactful childhood actually is. We become more aware of just how our childhood wounds affect our adult lives and how our childhood experiences influence our current behaviors and personality. Childhood lays the foundation for our whole life. As John Connolly, author of *The Book of Lost Things*, wrote: "For in every adult there dwells the child that was, and in every child there lies the adult that will be."

Every child *deserves* a safe and happy childhood. A healthy child becomes a healthy adult; several studies have proven this. Having a healthy childhood has numerous benefits such as more creativity, better problem-solving skills, better social skills, stronger resilience, higher academic performance, fewer behavioral problems, better overall health, and increased life satisfaction (Li, 2023). Unfortunately, many children do experience traumatic events. In fact, according to the

Substance Abuse and Mental Health Services Administration (2023), about 67% of children will have experienced at least one traumatic event in their life by age 16. The CDC (2022b) also states that in the United States alone, at least one in seven children have experienced abuse or neglect within the past year and that in 2020, as many as 1,750 children died because of it. Even these numbers are most likely underestimated since many cases of child abuse or neglect are left unreported.

Understanding Childhood Trauma

Experiencing traumatic events during our childhood can lead to unresolved trauma in our adulthood. Childhood trauma, according to the Illinois Childhood Trauma Coalition (n.d.), is defined as "the experience of an event by a child that is emotionally painful or distressful, which often results in lasting mental and physical effects." The word *trauma* is actually Greek for *wound*. As mentioned in its definition, childhood trauma can have long-term impacts on our health, well-being, and success. These wounds can be inflicted by parents, caregivers, or any person in a custodial role—such as a religious leader, a coach, or a teacher. The CDC shared four common types of abuse and neglect which are (2022a):

Physical abuse. Some examples of physical abuse are hitting, kicking, or shaking a child. With physical abuse, the perpetrator intentionally uses physical force which can result in physical harm or injury such as cuts, bruises, or broken bones. It is considered as the second most common form of child maltreatment. Aside from physical injuries, children who suffered from physical abuse can also develop traumatic stress, depression, or anxiety. It is believed that physical abuse often results from punishments within the child's home that simply goes too far or from a parent or caregiver lashing out in anger. Children are most often abused by a caregiver or someone they know. Some signs of physical abuse in children are injuries that have a pattern or don't align with a logical explanation, changing explanations as to what caused the injury, new injuries over the scar of healed ones, receiving no medical care, habitual absence or lateness to school, attempts to hide injuries through clothing, awkward movement or difficulty walking due to pain, and disclosure of physical abuse (Nationwide Children's, n.d.).

Sexual abuse. Some examples of sexual abuse are fondling, penetration, exposing a child to sexual acts, or sexual trafficking. With sexual abuse, the perpetrator forces or pressures a child into engaging in sexual activity for their own gratification or financial benefit. This involves both touching and non-touching behaviors. In 2018 alone, about 47,000 children were victims of sexual abuse in the United States. It is estimated that nearly 1 in 4 girls and 1 in 13 boys experience sexual abuse. Unfortunately, 91% of child sexual abuse is perpetrated by someone the victim knows (Prevent Child Abuse America, n.d.). Children who have been sexually abused are at an increased risk of falling victim to sexual exploitation, in which one abuser passes them around a network of abusers, further perpetrating the abuse. Some signs a child may be a victim of sexual abuse are negative changes in behavior, having nightmares or wetting the bed, fear or extreme dislike of a particular person, sexually inappropriate behavior or language use, health problems, or the presence of sexually transmitted diseases, difficulty concentrating at school, and giving hints about the abuse through their words or play (NHS, 2023).

Emotional abuse. This is sometimes also referred to as 'psychological' or 'verbal abuse'. Some examples of emotional abuse are name-calling, shaming, rejecting, threatening, isolating, and withholding love from a parent or a guardian. With emotional abuse, the perpetrator behaves in a way that harms a child's emotional well-being or self-worth. In 2022, during the pandemic, the CDC reported that more than half of U.S. high school students—55%—claimed they experienced emotional abuse in their homes (CDC, 2022a). A study revealed that childhood emotional abuse may be linked to problematic alcohol use later in life (Shin et al., 2015). Although emotional abuse may not seem as straightforward as physical or sexual abuse and, therefore, might be more difficult to grasp, Hilit Kletter—a child psychologist at Child and Adolescent Mental Health

Services—explains that it is just as damaging and that it "increases the risk for posttraumatic stress disorder, depression, anxiety, suicidal ideation, substance use, and chronic health conditions" (Chen, 2022). Some signs of emotional abuse are avoiding or running away from home, self-image and self-esteem issues, developmental delays, poor performance at school, constant anxiety or fear, increased negative behaviors, people-pleasing, and being withdrawn. The victim may also have feelings of worthlessness, being unwanted or unloved, guilt, and shame (Kids Helpline, 2023).

Neglect. Some examples of neglect are invalidating a child's feelings—or reacting inappropriately to them—and not providing the child with his or her basic needs such as food, housing, clothing, education, or medical care. With neglect, the child's primary guardians fail to meet the child's basic physical and emotional needs. In the United States, neglect is the most common reason for child maltreatment cases reported to child protective services (Stanford News, 2018). It is considered the most common form of child abuse. Neglect has four types: *Physical, educational, emotional,* and *medical.* Any child can suffer neglect, but there are some children that are considered at an increased risk. These are children who are born prematurely, have a disability, have challenging or complex health needs, have mental health problems, or are in foster care. Some parents or guardians may unintentionally neglect their children as well. Those who live in poverty—and are, therefore, already having a hard time providing themselves and their family the basic necessities—are at an increased risk (NSPCC, n.d.). However, we must remember that neglect *is* still a form of child abuse, as it can have deep and negative long-term effects on the child. Some signs that a child is neglected are if they are left hungry, dirty, without proper clothing or shelter, and if the child does not have adult supervision the majority of the time, as well as lack of health care.

Impact of Parenting on Childhood Trauma

There is no such thing as a "typical" abuser; research has shown us that. However, in over 80% of cases, the perpetrator of the abuse is the child's parents. Adults who have low self-esteem, poor emotional control, a history of also being abused, stress, financial problems, relationship problems, drug or alcohol problems, illness, depression, and misguided parenting beliefs are just some of the characteristics that make one more likely to abuse children. On the other hand, children who have a disability, poor grades, and chronic illnesses are some of the ones that are at an increased risk for child abuse (Children's Wisconsin, n.d.). That being said, it is extremely important to highlight that children are <u>never</u> responsible for being abused or neglected.

However, trauma is not always black and white. Even parents who are loving and devoted to their children can cause their children trauma. This may come as a shock, but it's true that abuse isn't always intentional. The way the child was brought up, or events that happened with their parents in childhood, could have long-lasting effects on the child. The sheer absence of a parental presence or the lack of engagement—which can amount to neglect over a period of time—often goes unnoticed and unaddressed. That is because there is no one huge painful incident causing the trauma. However, a child's attachment and relationship with their parents are also part of their basic needs. If this need is consistently unmet, it results in neglect, which can cause harm. To further demonstrate, here are some examples of neglect that are often unintentional and go unnoticed:

Lack of time spent with the child. Parents are tasked with a great deal. They are not only responsible for keeping a child safe and happy but also putting a roof above their heads and food on their table, as well as sending them to good schools. As they ensure that the financial aspect of the household is met, this may mean that the time they can spend with their child becomes limited. It could also be for a different reason that is natural or accidental, such as a parent having to live away from the child or a parent dealing with a serious illness. Whatever the reason is, spending time with children is important in order for a parent to form healthy, solid, and safe attachments with them. Spending time solely focused on children 24/7 is, of course, not always possible. A parent doesn't have to supervise their child every minute of the day, however. What I mean is that parents must carve out some time to engage children in activities they would both enjoy, where they can communicate and bond with each other. The time parents spend with their children will turn into a repertoire of memories the child will fall back upon in times of distress and challenges, and it will help them form secure relationships with themselves and others.

Lack of listening. When somebody is truly listening to us, we become more comfortable with expressing ourselves and effectively communicating our needs, thoughts, and feelings. This is the same, if not more important, for children too. However, listening requires a parent to be fully present at the moment, as it is not enough to simply hear what a child is saying. Being able to empathize and communicate with them so that they can identify their issues, emotions, or struggles is what children need. This can be difficult when a parent is extremely busy. However, if a child is not able to identify and express their emotions at an early age, they may carry that struggle with them as an adult.

Lack of consistency. Children need security and consistency. Part of that is knowing that they can rely on their parents for help and support. When parents do things sporadically, moodily, or without commitment to consistency, children may start believing that love is conditional and needs to be earned before they are deserving of it. Providing consistency to a child means sticking to a general predictable schedule, giving a heads up on any disruption from the routine, and including them in activities throughout the day. It could be something short like reading them a story before bed or being home for dinner with them every night. Consistent actions like this help children form their own ideas of what a secure relationship is like, and they will carry that knowledge with them into adulthood.

If you were able to relate to any of these, even though you believe that you've had a happy childhood, that is normal. Your parents could both love you and still give you trauma. The first step is in realizing that both of those things can be true and can exist at the same time. You can have good and loving parents while having childhood trauma. The two are not mutually exclusive. You can also love, forgive, or empathize with your parents and still acknowledge the fact that you will have to deal with the trauma you received, and that's okay too.

Signs of Lingering Childhood Trauma and Finding Professional Help

So, how does childhood trauma manifest in us as we're navigating adulthood? There are a few signs you may have lingering childhood trauma, these include event flashbacks or nightmares, trust issues, and self-destructive or risky behaviors. If you find yourself dealing with these issues for no apparent reason, you might have unresolved childhood trauma. Those who are dealing with trauma may also struggle to figure out their emotions. They may have sudden uncontrollable anger, anxiety, depression, and an inability to express their emotions. They also have the tendency to withdraw from other people or have trouble forming and keeping relationships (Institute For Advanced Psychiatry, n.d.).

Childhood trauma not only affects your mental and emotional health, but it can actually also have an impact on your physical health. A study published in the American Journal of Preventive Medicine states that the more adverse experiences a child has, and the more they are exposed to repeated trauma, the higher their risk of developing asthma, coronary heart disease, diabetes, and stroke (Gilbert et al., 2015). A review of 134 different research-based articles also concluded that children who are exposed to adverse experiences have a higher chance of developing other health conditions such as autoimmune diseases, pulmonary disease, cardiovascular disease, and cancer, as well as increasing levels of pain (Zarse et al., 2019).

Untreated childhood trauma can result in these issues long-term, so it's best to get help. Treatment can help you identify triggers, decrease symptoms, and develop healthy coping strategies in a safe and supportive environment. Some common treatments for childhood trauma include:

Cognitive processing therapy (CPT). This is a subtype of cognitive behavioral therapy (CBT) which teaches you how to change your thoughts so you can change how you feel. The goal is for you to evaluate upsetting thoughts and reframe the way you think and feel about them. The rationale behind this is that trauma can change the way we think and feel about ourselves and the world. There may be feelings of self-blame, or there may be an intense distrust or fear of the world. These thoughts may come from the trauma you experienced and may hold you back from enjoying life. CPT will help you learn better ways of thinking about your trauma and how to cope with these thoughts in a healthier way. CPT programs usually offer 12 weekly sessions, with the sessions being 60 to 90 minutes long each. Expect to feel discomfort in the beginning as you would have to face trauma-related memories and feelings by talking or writing about them. However, most people who have completed CPT find that the long-term benefits make the initial discomfort well worth it. CPT is considered one of the most effective types of treatment for trauma (U.S. Department of Veterans Affairs, 2022).

Trauma-focused cognitive behavioral therapy (TF-CBT). This method is also a subtype of CBT. TF-CBT focuses on evidence-based treatment for children and adolescents. Because the clients are young, TF-CBT often brings non-offending caregivers into treatment along with the child and incorporates principles found in family therapy. TF-CBT is treated mainly as an intervention. Often, the child and non-offending caregiver will have separate therapy sessions before advancing into joint sessions. Then, CBT techniques are used to help reframe thinking and learn to challenge thoughts of guilt and fear. Caregivers or family members, on the other hand, are taught how to deal with the trauma suffered by the child. This includes stress management, communication, and parenting techniques. TF-CBT is generally done short-term and involves between eight to 25 sessions (Psychology Today, 2022).

Eye movement desensitization and reprocessing (EMDR). EMDR is an interactive psychotherapy technique that uses repetitive eye movements to change the pattern of memories resulting from trauma. The theory behind the approach is that we experience post-traumatic stress because we don't process the trauma completely. Because of this, certain sights, sounds, words, or smells can trigger unprocessed memories, and the individual feels like they are re-experiencing the trauma. The EDMR approach aims to change how these memories are stored in our brains so that the trauma symptoms are reduced. How it usually goes is that an EMDR therapist will lead the patient through a series of side-to-side eye movements while recalling traumatic or triggering experiences in small segments. This is done repeatedly until the memories no longer cause the patient distress. Since its introduction in 1987, there have been a number of studies supporting EDMR's effectiveness (Gotter & Raypole, 2023).

Prolonged Exposure (PE) Therapy. This approach is sometimes referred to as 'flooding' and is another subset of CBT. With PE, patients are asked to repeat their trauma stories, as well as engage in take-home activities they would otherwise avoid because they trigger traumatic memories. The treatment would first tackle the least distressing traumas or memories until the patient can work their way up to the most distressing ones. These retellings are repeated until the patient feels more in control of their thoughts and feelings. PE usually takes place over three months (Sansom, 2023).

Tips for Healing Childhood Trauma

Healing childhood trauma as an adult is a daunting endeavor; however, it is possible and worth it. Childhood trauma should no longer dictate the rest of your life! To heal childhood trauma, you have to be intentional, patient, and kind to yourself. You can start healing your childhood trauma and reclaiming your life through the following ways:

Acknowledge what happened and recognize the trauma. A lot of victims of childhood trauma often deny or minimize the severity of the event. They can spend years running away from it. They can spend their lives blaming and guilting themselves for it. To start healing, you must face what happened exactly just as it happened. Then, you must recognize that you are a victim of childhood trauma and that the event is unfortunately a part of your reality. Again, even if you had a happy childhood and loving parents, you can still experience trauma. There is no need to deny or minimize your truth to protect others or because you love or understand them. This is about you, and how you heal moving forward.

Reclaim control. Childhood trauma can make us think, feel, and do things that seem to come out of nowhere once our wounds are triggered. Feelings of helplessness can carry well over into adulthood. Those who are suffering from trauma may feel like they are constantly the victim. However, victims are controlled by the past and the actions done by the perpetrator. That doesn't have to still be the case for you! You may never be able to erase your past, and there may always be a constant battle with it, but you have to remind yourself that YOU are in control of your present now. Identify the crutches and defenses you were forced to use as a child to navigate your trauma and replace them with healthier and more mature ways to cope. That's how you start to reclaim control and heal.

Seek support and avoid isolation. Withdrawing from others and isolating themselves is part of a trauma survivor's natural instinct. As we know, doing this only makes things more difficult. Connecting with other people, being heard, and having your feelings and experiences validated are a big part of not just healing, but of being human. Taking the first few steps towards healing may be triggering and you may feel as if everything has to get worse before it gets better. Do not isolate yourself from your loved ones during these tough times. Talk to your most-trusted person, your best friend, or even a medical professional. You may also want to consider joining a support group to find people who are on the same journey as you.

Take good care of your health. We all know now that our mental and emotional well-being is closely tied to our physical well-being.

That's why keeping yourself healthy is one of the best things you can do as you go through your healing journey. Having a healthy mind and body will help you cope with stress better. So, establish a daily routine wherein you will be able to get plenty of rest, eat a well-balanced diet, and exercise regularly. Most importantly, avoid using alcohol and drugs. These substances may have helped you cope before, but the relief they bring will always be temporary while the harm may not. Drugs and alcohol will inevitably worsen depression and anxiety symptoms, as well as further isolate you from people who care about you. We are now trying to establish healthier and more sustainable ways of coping, so just say "no" to them.

Replace bad habits with good ones. What we had just discussed about using alcohol or drugs as crutches is a good example of a bad habit. These are the things we do, sometimes impulsively, that temporarily relieve the pain or anxiety to the detriment of our own health and well-being. Although these coping methods may have worked for a while, they have to be replaced by healthy ones for us to fully and sustainably heal. Most of the therapy options we have previously discussed have the same goal, so a therapist or support group can be a great help in providing you with the tools necessary to make a change. Meditation and journaling are other good habits that you can use to replace the bad ones. It can be difficult at first without these old crutches but keep working on it. You deserve to heal without ruining yourself in the process.

Be patient with yourself. Getting to the root cause of your trauma, being at peace with it, tearing down defense mechanisms, and establishing healthy ways of coping is a lot, especially for someone who is already struggling. Be patient with yourself and take it one day at a time. Remind yourself that this is a marathon, not a sprint and that you owe it to yourself to try. Honor the hard work, the struggles, and the feelings throughout the journey. Focus on the victories, no matter how small they seem. It gets better eventually; that much is true.

Also, if you are not yet ready to get professional help, there are simple activities you can do daily to help promote healing. Fortunately, you are already familiar with a lot of these! Some activities you can engage in to help you heal include meditation, journaling, empathizing and speaking kindly to yourself, nourishing your body with comforting and healthy foods, spending time in nature, gentle exercises or yoga, slowing down, resting, and setting boundaries (Huber, 2019). You can also engage in these activities concurrent to therapy.

· ♥ · ♥ · ♥ · ♥ · ♥ ·

Overcoming Childhood Trauma Story You Need To Learn From Today

In a post for his blog in Medium.com, Dr. Ibrahim Kurdieh shared the story of how he overcame his childhood wounds. He wrote about the memory that sticks out most for him which was when he was about eight years old. His parents and siblings were not around, and he was alone in their house, cozy under a blanket in his bed. Just as he was beginning to doze off, he heard a banging noise on the window. It was his father furiously beating the window with his fist. It seemed like they had been outside for a while, waiting to be let in because they had forgotten to take their key with them.

When Dr. Kurdieh opened the door to let them in, his father charged at him, pushed him to the ground, and started beating him. Dr. Kurdieh's mother was begging his father to stop. This commotion was all because his father had waited. He shared that these beatings occurred on a regular basis. Dr. Kurdieh was a victim of child abuse, and he suffered from trauma because of it.

He stated that memory alone took him years to recover from, and once he started working on healing his trauma, he had other traumatic memories suddenly resurface. Now a doctor, Dr. Kurdieh advises that childhood trauma patients subconsciously bring the traumatic emotions into their daily lives. These emotions are grief, anger, fear, shame, or numbness. However, he highlighted that most of the fears that bring about these emotions are already in the past; hence, people with childhood trauma are barking up the wrong tree when they bring these feelings with them in the present. He shared that to overcome his trauma, he had to go on a "hero's journey," which included healing his body, mind, heart, and spirit, as well as learning how to identify and set boundaries.

"The path out of developmental trauma and into a healthy emotional life is a long and hard one," he wrote. "Nonetheless, it is well worth the effort as the alternative is more misery and further suffering" (Kurdieh, 2019).

Chapter Activity: Healing Journal Prompts

In this chapter, you learned about childhood trauma and how even the most well-intentioned parents can leave us childhood wounds. If you need help identifying your wounds, trauma, or how you're feeling, you can ask yourself the following questions to help you reflect. You can also write your answers down in your journal. Remember, this is for your eyes only, so you can be as honest with your thoughts and feelings as you can. If you are sad or angry, write it down. If someone wronged you as a child, you don't have to hide it. As discussed, one of the first steps of healing is recognizing the trauma. Here are the questions:

In what ways do I self-sabotage?
What negative beliefs do I have about myself and the world?
Where do these negative beliefs come from?
What situations are difficult for me to be in?
What is blocking me from having an accurate and clear perception of myself?
Who did I get the belief that 'I am not important' from?
What other unhelpful beliefs or ideas about myself do I have, and from whom did I get them from?
In what ways do I feel like the victim?
Do I let others dictate how I feel?

Do I believe that I am not worthy of anything good?
Have I ever set healthy boundaries in my relationships?
What mistakes do I keep making and repeating, and why?
Do I react appropriately, or do I either go overboard or shut down?
What triggers my negative or unhelpful behaviors?
Does putting up barriers make me feel safe, and why?

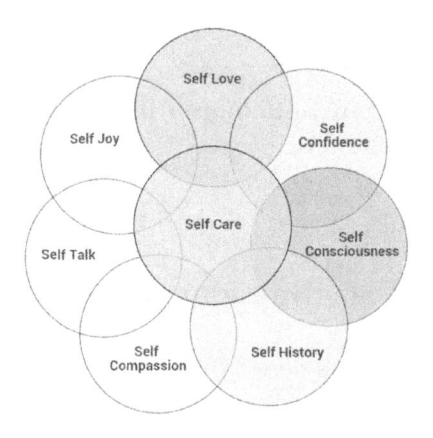

Practicing Self-Compassion

People are like stained-glass windows. They sparkle and shine when the sun is out, but when the darkness sets in, their true beauty is revealed only if there is a light from within. -Elisabeth Kubler-Ross

Did you know there are studies that show that, in general, women are better at empathizing and showing compassion than men? In a study involving participants from 36 countries, women on average scored significantly higher in cognitive empathy than men did. The study further states that "there wasn't a single country in which men scored better, on average than women" (Christensen, 2022). There are many possible reasons for this. It could be how our brains biologically differ from men, as discussed in chapter two, or it could be because men and women experience and express compassion differently. It has been observed that we as a society collectively thinks of compassion through maternal and nurturing terms, whereas men tend to express compassion through protective behaviors (Seppala, 2013). Whatever the case may be, the takeaway is not which gender is more compassionate, but that there are many beautiful forms in which we can experience and express compassion, and that we as women have the ability to give so much empathy not only to others but to ourselves too—*as long as we learn self-compassion.*

Understanding Self-Compassion

First, let's discuss what self-compassion is and why it's important. We already briefly touched upon it in previous chapters, but one definition of self-compassion is "the ability to turn understanding, acceptance, and love inward" (Good Therapy, 2019). Compassion itself is our ability to express empathy, love, and concern towards other people, so self-compassion is simply directing all of these positive emotions toward our own selves. Unfortunately, many compassionate people have a hard time practicing self-compassion. There are various reasons for this, but it could be because of not wanting to appear weak, not wanting to indulge in self-pity or self-indulgence, or not being able to fully connect with one's own painful feelings. Gender norms may also affect women's difficulty in showing self-compassion as women are socially assigned the 'caregiver' role, with self-sacrificing acts emphasized and expected.

Dr. Kristin Neff, the leading researcher in the growing field of self-compassion, explains that self-compassion has three elements. These are (Neff, n.d.):

Self-kindness vs. self-judgment. Self-judgment is our tendency to mercilessly judge and criticize ourselves for our perceived weaknesses, flaws, inadequacies, and mistakes. This leads to a lot of shame, guilt, and even anger pointed towards ourselves. Self-compassionate people recognize their imperfections and accept that failing and falling short in life are inevitable. Because of this, they are able to be more gentle and forgiving of themselves, and they are also more open to criticism and asking for forgiveness. Self-compassionate people accept their reality with sympathy and kindness; therefore, they are able to extend the same to others.

Common humanity vs. isolation. As previously discussed, some people's first instinct when in a tough situation or when faced with pain is to withdraw and isolate themselves. This could further lead to self-judgment, self-pity, and overall negative rumination. Also, when we are stressed or when our mental health is at its lowest, we tend not to think clearly and logically. Hence, we may start having this irrational belief that we are the only person suffering and making mistakes. Of course, we know that that is simply not true and that failing and making mistakes are universal experiences. That is why self-compassion involves having a sense of common humanity, in which one recognizes that life and humans are not perfect and that we all fall down sometimes. Because of this, they are able to handle difficult emotions better, are more hopeful, and are more willing to seek out support from others.

Mindfulness vs. over-identification. Over-identification of feelings means that we place so much focus and importance on our, often negative, emotions that we let them take over our identities. For example, someone who may be struggling with depressive symptoms for a while may start believing that this is simply the way they are and that they are always going to suffer. Instead of them thinking, "I feel awful," they may think, "I'm an awful person." Self-compassion requires us to have a more balanced approach to our emotions, in a way that we are still able to process and acknowledge them, but we are also not exaggerating or magnifying them. This requires mindfulness and a non-judgmental, receptive state of mind. We cannot ignore painful feelings; however, we also cannot let them rule our actions and our lives.

Myths About Self-Compassion

As mentioned, some people—mostly women—find it easy to be compassionate toward others but find it difficult to extend the same grace toward themselves. That is because, similar to self-love, there are a lot of misconceptions surrounding self-compassion that we subconsciously believe.

One of which is that self-compassion is equivalent to self-pity. No one likes feeling pitiful and that is why people tend to avoid looking inward in fear that they will find themselves in that position. However, self-compassion actually *is* the antidote to self-pity. When we practice self-compassion, we are more willing to accept our difficult experiences and, therefore, have less tendency to whine about it. In fact, a study conducted by Filip Raes at the University of Leuven concluded that self-compassionate people are less likely to get swallowed up by self-pitying thoughts. They brood and ruminate less, and report fewer anxiety and depression symptoms (Raes, 2010).

Another myth is that self-compassion equals weakness. People who take on caregiving, nurturing, or dependable roles often avoid looking inward for fear of letting their guard down and "crumbling" from weakness. They tend to believe that they have to be self-reliant and "strong" all the time because that's who they are. However, this thinking only results in unaddressed emotions that would resurface if continued to be left unchecked. Paradoxically, what these people are trying to avoid may actually be the answer to their problems. Researchers have found that people who displayed more self-compassion when talking about difficult experiences—divorce in this study—evidenced better psychological adjustment in the long run (Janson, 2011). Studies like this show that it's not what we go through in life, but how we relate to ourselves during tough times—*whether we see ourselves as an ally or an enemy*—that determines our ability to successfully cope.

Another myth that is possibly the biggest misconception out there is that self-compassion will make us complacent and, therefore, less likely to push ourselves to do better. The idea behind this belief is that if we don't criticize ourselves for not meeting our often-impossible standards, we would automatically succumb to accepting "mediocrity" in ourselves. This great-or-nothing approach rarely works. Just like in parenting, using constant criticisms to motivate a child only causes more harm than good. In fact, a study done by University of California researchers (Breines & Chen, 2012) showed that self-compassion actually increases self-improvement motivation. They did this by asking undergraduate students to write themselves a compassionate letter about a recent action that they felt guilty about. They asked this set of participants to write the letter as if they were writing to a friend. The results showed that the participants who were asked to be more self-compassionate were more willing to apologize and were more committed to not repeating the same mistake. Therefore, self-compassion is not a vehicle for us to avoid self-accountability. In fact, self-compassion actually strengthens it.

Similarly, another myth surrounding self-compassion is that it is highly narcissistic. According to the Merriam-Webster dictionary (n.d.-d), a narcissist is "an extremely self-centered person who has an exaggerated sense of self-importance." This distorted view of self-importance most likely comes from issues with self-esteem, and self-esteem is different from self-compassion. Although the two are strongly linked when it comes to our psychological well-being, self-esteem requires an evaluation of our self-worth, while self-compassion requires no judgment or evaluation at all. Self-compassion mostly focuses on riding the waves of human existence and extending kindness and acceptance to ourselves no matter what we are going through. Self-compassion is also important in building up our self-esteem; however, it does not result in us being "better" than anyone. On the contrary, and as previously discussed, self-compassion requires us to acknowledge that we are all flawed and imperfect. That is the exact opposite of narcissism.

Lastly, just like with self-love, there's this myth that self-compassion is inherently selfish. Again, this stems from our views about what compassion actually looks like and society's emphasis on self-sacrifice being one of the main indicators of compassion in action. That is why when we extend compassion towards ourselves and make choices that put our own well-being first, it can appear as being selfish or uncaring to other people. This is especially true for women who are taught and expected by society to be selfless caregivers and nurturers but are rarely taught how to care for themselves. Even with the rise of feminism, the idea that women should be selfless hasn't really gone away. For example, even though women now have the opportunity to thrive in their own careers, they are still expected to be the ultimate nurturers at home. However, it's time that we change this idea that we are only modest, self-effacing, caring, and successful women when we are making sacrifices or when we treat ourselves badly for the sake of our loved ones. As you know by now, you can be kind and still say "no." You can be a compassionate person and still put your own well-being first. You can be a successful woman without being everyone's caregiver. The irony is that self-compassion actually allows us to be more considerate of others. That's because, as we have learned, when our cup is full, it's easier to give. Letting our cup run empty and being unkind towards ourselves actually only gets in the way of relating to other people. In fact, a growing body of research supports that self-compassion helps us sustain the act of caring for others and makes the act more fulfilling (Neff, 2015).

Learning to Release Shame

Have you ever felt like there is something inherently wrong with you? Toxic shame, or the feeling that we're worthless, is not something we are born with. We pick it up from other people's actions towards us, especially during childhood or teenage years when we are most vulnerable. We pick it up whenever someone would treat us poorly or would make us feel like we are difficult to love. It happens when we take the awful treatment we receive and turn it into a belief about ourselves. For example, if as a child, we came home with a failing mark on a test and our parents reacted in a way that blames us or makes us feel as if we were stupid, we might start agreeing with their criticisms and start harboring shame. Whereas this can be prevented if our parents would have reacted in a more compassionate, helpful, and understanding way. Toxic shame is one of the major roadblocks one can have when trying to practice self-compassion.

Guilt and shame are often used interchangeably, but they are not exactly the same. We feel guilt when we know we've done something wrong, which can be helpful in our relationships and in upholding our integrity. Guilt keeps us aligned with our moral compass. Shame, on the other hand, is when we believe that we are simply 'not enough,' usually because we've been told so constantly by other people. Shame affects our self-esteem deeply, and our confidence and self-image suffer because of it. To further differentiate, guilt is the voice inside of us that says, "What you did was wrong, make it right." Whereas shame tells us, "You are a bad person because of what you did."

Shame can last for a few hours to a few days, but it transforms into toxic shame when you start carrying it with you throughout your life. It results in negative self-talk that stays with us—*think your mean inner critic*—which can then lead us into believing that we're not worthy of love or goodness. These feelings of unworthiness, as we now know, can be extremely damaging to our mental and physical well-being. Unfortunately, shame makes us hide parts of ourselves from others while magnifying the 'shadowy' or 'ugly' parts of ourselves internally. For example, if we are ashamed of our body and the way it looks, the tendency is to hide our body. Since we never really let that part of ourselves surface and see the light of day, the wound of shame within us never gets the chance to heal.

How To Deal With Shame and Guilt

Shame and guilt are universal emotions and, as we now know, even negative emotions have purpose and help us survive. They are not necessarily unhealthy on their own. However, the context and judgment we place on them, as well as the ways we choose to cope, are what can make these feelings toxic. The immediate reaction we tend to have when faced with shame and guilt is to bury it, hide it, or pretend it never happened. Doing so gives these emotions power over us. Also, suppressing any emotion, in general, has been proven to be bad for us. Long-term continual suppression of emotions can have negative psychological and physical effects such as anxiety, depression, and other stress-related illnesses. As we also know by now, it can lead us to self-medicate through the use of alcohol or drugs (Elsig, 2022). Because of this, the first step to dealing with shame and guilt healthily is to do the exact opposite: Bring them to light! Here are some tips on how you can do exactly that:

Separate who you are from what you've done. We are bound to make mistakes because we are human and, therefore, imperfect. We know this by now. That means we're going to do things that we're going to regret, and that regret may haunt us. However, just because you messed up, doesn't mean you yourself are messed up. Practice looking at your mistakes objectively, no matter how terrible they are. For example, if you hurt someone—whether intentional or unintentional—accept that you did hurt someone but refrain from believing that you are 'a horrible person who hurts people.' Use "I did..." not "I am..." statements. Reflect and use these experiences to improve. Use what you've gone through as motivation to do better next time because *you can* do better. You are not meant to be stuck repeating the same mistakes. Have faith in yourself and know that these experiences have value and that you are still a good person who will only keep learning and growing.

Empathize with the real motivation behind your actions. Once you've learned to separate your actions from your identity, you can start looking into the real motivations behind your actions. We really do unintentionally hurt people sometimes, and we do things with one intention in mind, but things don't translate or happen the way we want them to. Maybe we acted out of anger, or maybe an unhealed childhood wound was triggered which made us impulsive. Either way, getting to the bottom of the 'why' of our actions and coming to terms with it is necessary to learn lessons and improve ourselves. Also, no matter what reason we uncover, it's important to show ourselves a little empathy. Again, you can think of yourself as a friend. When a friend messes up, more often than not, we give them the benefit of the doubt and try hard to see where they are coming from. We also don't make them feel bad about their character. We simply accept the situation as it is: A mistake. Tell yourself what you would tell a friend, that it's going to be okay and that mistakes don't make you a bad person.

Do better next time. They say that an apology is incomplete if there is no positive change afterward. The same is true when dealing with guilt and shame. The only healthy way to move forward, after you've dissected what happened, is if you truly learn from it so that you can do better next time. If a negative experience makes you a better person, then you at least transform it into something useful. In this way, shame and guilt have a purpose and that is to motivate us to grow as people. Mistakes can be wise teachers if we let them—even if they make us feel unpleasant for a while.

Share your shame even if it hurts. It may even be more important to share your shame *especially* when it hurts. As we've discussed, repressed emotions affect us negatively physically and mentally. Unfortunately, shame and guilt make you want to hide or pretend as if things never happened. We have to fight against this counterintuitive urge and remind ourselves that it's actually by sharing what we are afraid of the most, that we actually receive the love and support we need. If you are finding it hard to believe, consider that this is the cornerstone of therapy. In therapy, you will be required to confront your negative feelings. Only then can you learn how to cope in healthy ways. The same is true with guilt and shame. We have to face them head-on so that we can move on.

Choose your shame, choose your values. Again, feelings of guilt and shame can serve as wise teachers, especially when determining what values we align ourselves with. For example, if you feel shame for not wearing the right clothes at an event, you might need to look at why you seem to value other people's judgment or your physical appearance so much. On the other hand, if you feel shame for canceling on a friend, you might realize that you value being a good friend as someone that can be relied on. In this way, we can use shame to tell us things about ourselves that we may not be consciously aware of. Then, we can start choosing better values, which in turn liberates us from the unnecessary shame that comes from our previously held poor values. Remember that our values determine our shame. So, if we don't like what brings us shame, it may be time to reconsider our values.

Self-Forgiveness

Now that you know a lot more about shame and guilt, it's time to discuss self-forgiveness, which is another important component of self-compassion. The official definition of 'forgiving' in the Merriam-Webster dictionary (n.d.-b) is "to give up resentment." It's the deliberate decision to let go of anger, resentment, and the need for retribution. If you are still struggling with self-compassion, you may find yourself being able to forgive others easily, while not being able to forgive yourself. But why is that? Why is forgiving ourselves so hard to do?

Well, it's probably because we were just never taught how! We've always been taught how to forgive others when we were children, but how to forgive ourselves was rarely mentioned. As a result, it can be a struggle to move on during times when we feel like we've let ourselves down. When someone disappoints us, it's easy to pinpoint how we feel, and it's usually anger. In a way, our anger even helps keep our self-image intact because we would have felt like we stood our ground and drew our own boundaries. When we mess up, however, it usually means that we went against our own values, and that brings up more complicated feelings than just anger. Beating ourselves up can even make us feel better because it convinces us that we take our past mistakes seriously. It is easy to get trapped in a spiral of self-blame, pity, and shame, especially if we haven't learned how to tame our mean inner critic yet. These feelings are neither productive nor healthy.

On the other hand, when we learn to become more compassionate with ourselves, self-forgiveness tends to come more easily—and vice versa! When we learn to put our shortcomings in perspective, we are able to move past them easily and even become better people afterward. Self-forgiveness is good for us in a lot of ways, this includes:

Improved mental and emotional health. Repressed negative thoughts and feelings can exacerbate stress, anxiety, and depressive symptoms. Self-forgiveness comes with letting these negative emotions go. When we free ourselves from internal turmoil, we are able to take better care of our emotional and psychological health.

Increased productivity. Research from Stanford University showed that people who practice self-forgiveness have "higher levels of success, productivity, focus, and concentration" (BeWell Stanford, 2019). When we either dwell or minimize our mistakes, and try to continue on as if nothing happened, we lose the opportunity to move on from it. Therefore, lingering feelings may distract us. Self-forgiveness helps us let go of these lingering emotions so that we can have more focus and energy to spend on more productive endeavors.

Reduced cognitive dissonance. Cognitive dissonance is the psychological discomfort we feel after doing something "wrong" or something that goes against our values. The discomfort comes from two conflicting beliefs. For example, we may identify us a good person, but when we inevitably mess up and end up hurting someone, this may clash with that identity and threaten our sense of self—*if we're not self-aware*. Cognitive dissonance can leave us feeling as if we are not ourselves, which can lead to us acting out of character. Self-forgiveness reduces cognitive dissonance because it allows us to accept our shortcomings without tying them to our identities. When we view mistakes as an inevitable part of being human, it is easier for us to accept that we are still good people who are still deserving of love and compassion, even if we mess up sometimes.

Decreased impostor syndrome. As previously discussed, impostor syndrome comes from low self-esteem and the pressure to be perfect. When we practice self-forgiveness, we let go of that impossible expectation and instead adopt a growth mindset, also known as a 'learning mindset.' With a growth mindset, we accept that we are perpetually learning and growing and, therefore, can never be perfect. Growth often comes from being able to learn from past mistakes and, therefore, requires self-forgiveness. When we are able to forgive ourselves, we are able to see past 'failures' as opportunities, and this allows us to let go of the need to be perfect and, therefore, reduces impostor syndrome.

Improved physical health. We already know that letting go of repressed emotions can improve our physical help, but self-forgiveness specifically also has a positive impact. A meta-analysis involving papers from 17 countries and more than 26,000 participants revealed that practicing self-forgiveness is associated with improved heart rate, blood pressure, and overall heart health. The review also noted reduced pain and cortisol levels. This is on top of the psychological benefits that self-forgiveness also gives us (Rasmussen et al., 2019).

A lot of the ways we practice self-compassion also help with self-forgiveness. That includes accepting that we are imperfect, getting to the root of why we're upset with ourselves and the motivations behind our actions, and repairing what we can, as well as doing better in the future. The most challenging part of self-forgiveness is finding a way to close the door on whatever happened. Whatever you choose to do after you mess up—whether you decide to apologize or not—you have to learn how to move on from it before you can truly let go and heal. No matter how painful it might still be, it won't do you any good to keep dissecting the situation. At a certain point, you have to take a deep breath and choose to close the door on it.

Remember, your own forgiveness depends solely on you. This may seem daunting, but it also means that you are in control and that you truly can cope with the feelings of helplessness, shame, or guilt that you may be struggling with. All you have to do is to look within and have the courage to allow yourself to be human. Life is too short to keep punishing yourself.

Exercises for Practicing Self-Compassion

Now that you have a good grasp of self-compassion, it's time for me to share some practical tips that you can actually apply in your day-to-day life. Self-compassion, like everything else we've discussed so far, takes consistent practice. Thankfully, there are some easy exercises you can do every day to help you do just that.

Some of them you are already familiar with, such as keeping a gratitude journal, taking care of your physical health, practicing self-care, and talking to yourself as if you are talking to a friend. Other exercises you can do are:

Take self-compassion breaks. Take some time out of your day to schedule being compassionate with yourself, we can call it a "self-compassion break." You can do this when you're trying to move on from a difficult situation…or even when you're not! During these breaks, reflect on what is causing you stress, whether it's an old wound or something that just happened that day. Then, acknowledge the feeling and tell yourself that you are giving yourself a moment to allow space for your feelings. Feel your feelings; cry them out or even verbalize them. You can declare out loud that you're hurt, stressed, or sorry. Once you've let yourself grieve, remind yourself that this is a universal human experience and that you are not alone. Tell yourself that other people feel the same way sometimes too, and everyone struggles. Put your hands over your heart and be mindful of your heartbeat and your warmth. You can also start to pat yourself as if you are comforting a friend. Remind yourself that you are alive, and these feelings are temporary. Then, think about what you need. Is it strength? Is it patience? Is it forgiveness? Once you've figured it out, ask yourself permission to do just that. Then, give yourself what you need. For example, if you need forgiveness, ask yourself: "May I forgive myself?" Follow it up with, "Yes, I forgive myself."

Give yourself a supportive touch. Touch activates our parasympathetic nervous system which helps us calm down and feel safe. Research shows that physical touch releases oxytocin in our brains, which gives us a sense of calm and comfort. It also lowers our heart rate and blood pressure, as well as lessens depression, anxiety, and pain. It even gives our immune systems a boost (Holland, 2018)! That's why when a loved one pats us on the back or gives us a hug, we feel a sense of relief, but did you know that you can do these to yourself too? It may seem awkward at first but try it out. You can do what's called the 'hand-on-heart' position which is exactly how it sounds.

When you feel distressing emotions taking over, take three deep breaths and gently place your hand over your heart. Focus on the warmth of your palm, your heartbeat, and the steady rise and fall of your chest. Linger with this feeling until you feel comforted. Other supportive touch positions are One hand on your cheek, cradling your face with both hands, gently stroking your arms, crossing your arms and giving yourself a gentle squeeze, placing your hand on your stomach, one hand over your stomach and one over your hand, and cupping one hand in the back of your lap. Think of it as if you are physically comforting your best friend. It's a quick, subtle, and straightforward way of showing compassion for ourselves.

Visualize. We are all now familiar with the power of visualization, so think of the most compassionate person you know. How do you feel whenever you talk to them? How do they usually interact with other people? What kind of words do they say? How do they usually react? What about them makes them comforting from your perspective? Then, imagine yourself being like them too! Visualize that you are that kind of person and that you are someone who has the ability to be compassionate towards yourself. If you can't think of anyone in your life, you can think of a public figure or even a fictional character you love.

Write it out and burn it. We tend to carry so much shame, guilt, and regret within us. In fact, we do it so much that, sometimes, it can seem impossible to even know how to start letting them all go. It's even more difficult because these thoughts and feelings are inside of us. That's why one thing you can do is tie these negative emotions with an *actual* act of letting go. Write about all of the trauma, regrets, fear, guilt, and shame on a piece of paper. Write about the person you no longer are or no longer wish to be. Then, go somewhere safe where you can throw what you've written into the fire. Honor your feelings as you watch it burn and allow yourself to let go of all that you've written. Bid it goodbye, and tell yourself that you are now free from those burdens—kind of like a phoenix rising from the ash of that fire; isn't that cool?

Self-Compassion Story You Need To Learn From Today

Michelle Becker, a therapist, and educator, shared her experience with a client in a blog post for the Center for Mindful Self-Compassion Organization's website. In the post, she wrote about Hanna (not her client's real name) and how, on their first therapy session, Hanna talked about her anger at her partner for 50 minutes straight. She shared many stories, but the root of all of the issues was that her partner never seemed to take her needs into account. Hanna shared that everything about their life revolved around his needs and that her needs were always overlooked. Michelle saw how genuinely angry and hurt Hanna was, so she asked Hanna what it's been like for her. Hanna didn't want to go there, however. She was much more comfortable talking about her flawed partner than about herself and her own experience. Hanna was adamant that her partner needed to change.

Michelle said that Hanna's main need at that moment was *to be seen*. However, it didn't seem like Hanna was even seeing Hanna. She only wanted to talk about her partner's wrongdoings but didn't really want to put a spotlight on *herself*. In their second session, Michelle knew she needed to try something different. At some point, she told Hanna, "There is someone on the other side of things that is really hurting and yet isn't getting any attention—no attention from your partner and no attention from us either, and that person is you."

Hanna was stunned because it was true. Even in her own therapy session, they were focused on everybody else aside from her. Michelle said she noticed Hanna's anger turn into sadness, and at long last, Hanna joined the room for the first time. It was only then that they were able to explore how awful it felt for Hanna to consistently feel invisible. As they looked deeper into that, Hanna realized that it was actually much bigger than just one relationship. Most of her relationships were focused on others to the exclusion of herself. Digging deeper, they realized that the root of this issue was that as Hanna grew up, no one seemed to see or consider her needs. So, this was the way Hanna learned how to survive: To behave in ways that make other people happy and to hide her own pain.

Michelle and Hanna started working on getting past this childhood defense mechanism that was obviously no longer serving her in adulthood. They first worked on Hanna, acknowledging her own needs and giving her own self the attention and care she desperately needed from others. Hanna needed to feel seen, and she had to learn how to give that to herself first. When Hanna learned how to be more mindful of herself, that was when she started taking care of herself in ways that she needed. She got familiar with her emotions, and she fully experienced her sadness and anger for the first time. She started reclaiming a part of herself that she suppressed all her life. She learned how to channel her negative emotions in healthy ways, and now that Hanna knew who she was, she was able to show up fully in her relationships and let her partner get to know the true her.

Seeing more clearly allowed Hanna to heal from the pains of her past, as well as help her set boundaries. And that is how self-compassion fosters healthy relationships. Wrapping up Hanna's story, Michelle said, "When we open with curiosity and acceptance to our own experience, we also move from focusing on needing our loved ones to see us to seeing ourselves, moving out of the dependent state we were in as children and into the empowered state of adulthood (Becker, 2023)."

Chapter Activity: A Letter To Burn

Now, we're going to write ourselves a letter with all the feelings, thoughts, and beliefs we want to let go of. In the end, I encourage you to read the entirety of what you wrote at least once before burning it. Ensure that you are lighting a fire in a safe place. If unsure, ask someone for a second opinion or check with a professional. If you don't feel like using fire, you can also rip the letter to shreds or crumple it and throw it as far as you can! Let's start! Here are the steps:
    1. Using pen and paper, describe an event when you felt unwelcome or distressing emotions. It could be something that happened either in the past or something that just happened within the

day.

2. Now, write a letter to yourself as though you were writing to a friend. For example, you can start with, "I am sad because…" Write down whatever comes to your mind, as no one else is going to read this. Use this letter as a safe space to pour your heart out.

3. At the end of the letter, write what you need. Is it forgiveness? Maybe acceptance? Some reassurance that you're going to be alright? Or maybe all of the above? You can go ahead and write down whatever you need at the moment.

4. Once you've identified the situation and your needs, finish the letter with a message of compassion, acceptance, and forgiveness. Write down that you are ready to let this negative event go now. You can also write about how you're going to move forward and what steps you are going to take to grow from the situation.

5. Most importantly, read back what you've written. When we see our emotions physically separate from us, it's great practice for being able to do that internally too—looking at our emotions objectively. That way, we too can easily share our feelings with others. Think of your words on paper as your vulnerable side that's living outside of your body at the moment.

6. Lastly, you must let go of the paper. Do not bury it, hide it, or stick it in between the pages of your journal. You must either crumple it and throw it away, cut it into shreds, or—the most symbolic choice—burn it.

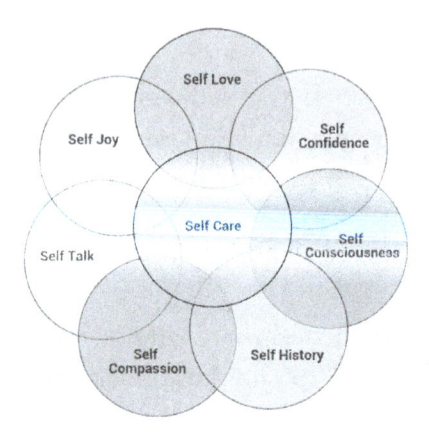

The Way You Talk to Yourself

The more man meditates upon good thoughts, the better will be his world and the world at large. -Confucius

What's the last thought you've had? Was it you talking to yourself inside your head? If yes, then you have just encountered your inner voice. In previous chapters, we've touched upon our inner critic and learned about the importance of befriending it. In this chapter, we'll dig deeper into the topic and talk about the different ways we negatively talk to ourselves, as well as how we can change that. The concept of an inner voice has been discussed for centuries by both philosophers and psychologists alike. But did you know that in psychology, the voice in our heads officially has two categories? Yes, there's the *internal monologue* and the *internal dialogue*.

The internal monologue is what we are referring to when we say 'inner voice' and is essentially the voice you hear when you, for example, tell yourself to, "remember to buy some milk." It's the result of certain brain mechanisms which allow us to "hear" ourselves talk inside our heads without having to actually speak. While most people have them, what's interesting is that not everyone does. This doesn't mean that people who don't experience internal monologue don't have thoughts because they do! It's just that it's not the same type of inner speech wherein you can "hear" your voice in your head expressing a thought. Researchers aren't exactly sure why some people hear themselves and some people don't, but it's been theorized that it may have something to do with the formation of the brain's dorsal language stream during early childhood (Geva & Fernyhough, 2019). The way we talk to ourselves internally also varies. Some hear their thoughts verbally, whereas others think more visually (Williams et al., 2008).

The internal dialogue, on the other hand, is a little more complicated. It's what you are experiencing when you replay a scenario in your head—thinking about what was said, what should have been said, and how everything played out. It's also what happens when you imagine yourself talking to someone else, such as having an argument with them or creating a totally fictional exchange. It's often compared to longer exchanges between several characters—kind of like a movie all inside our heads! Experts think that not everyone has the ability to have an internal dialogue (Plackett, 2021).

Our internal monologues and dialogues are actually a product of a healthy mind. For example, our inner voice can help us prepare for a presentation or it can help us make plans. One of the most common ways it can negatively affect us, however, is when we talk to ourselves too much and too critically. Enter... the *mean inner critic*, who we are all extremely familiar with by now.

Recognizing Negative Self-Talk

We also all know by now that one of our goals is to befriend our mean inner critic so that it stops being so hateful all the time. When our mean inner critic takes the driver's seat, it immediately jumps into patterns of negative self-talk. Fortunately, our mean inner critic is predictable, which means we can watch out for its tricks, and we can change its course. Here are some patterns to watch out for to identify when your mean inner critic is in the driver's seat:

Filtering. There is often both a positive and a negative aspect that comes out of a situation. Filtering is when our brain chooses to zero in on the negative aspects while simultaneously filtering out all the positive ones. One example of this is when you have so much to do you can only think of what's next. You may have checked five things off your to-do list already by noon and may have even received thanks or compliments from other people, but you are unable to process all of that because you're focusing on the five more tasks that are left undone. This is also what happens when we have a bad moment during the day, and we let it ruin the whole day. For example, you may have missed your alarm clock and it made you late for work. When you fall into a filtering thought pattern, you may focus on the imperfect morning and not notice that there have been so many positive things that have already happened after that. When filtering is done constantly, life can definitely seem unfair, and it becomes difficult to look forward to the day-to-day.

Personalizing. In a previous chapter, we touched upon the need to separate who we are from what we've done. Our minds have the tendency to fall into that pattern when something bad happens, and that pattern is actually called 'personalizing.' This is when we use "I am..." statements instead of objectively looking at a situation. An example of this is when your friend cancels out on you because they're suddenly stuck at work. Instead of accepting that these things happen, and you can reschedule, your brain may immediately take the cancellation personally. You may think that your friend canceled because he simply didn't want to be around you, and that must mean there's something wrong with you. Basically, it's when you automatically blame yourself for anything bad that happens, and we already know how bad self-blame is for us. Whenever you catch yourself falling into this pattern, look at the evidence. In the same example, your friend gave a valid excuse that has nothing to do with you. Hence, there is no need to jump to that negative conclusion and take things so personally.

Catastrophizing. You might have already guessed from the name, but yes, catastrophizing is our brain's tendency to anticipate the worst-case scenario. I'm sure we're all familiar with this. This is when our negative self-talk is just so loud it prevents us from even trying, or when we make a mistake, we automatically think that we won't be able to recover. For example, you may have forgotten to submit an important report at work, and after realizing what happened, you may immediately start thinking that you're going to get fired. Then, you may start spiraling and think that you're going to go bankrupt and homeless after you lose your job. Another example is staying stuck in a job that you hate because when you think of quitting or looking for another job, your inner critic immediately tells you that you won't find anything better and that you're simply going to fail. You could fall into this pattern of thinking even though there is no actual reason for you to expect the worst. Your boss may have always been understanding. Your skills and experiences may fit another job's requirements. When we catastrophize, we let fear and worry rule our lives.

Polarizing. When we polarize, we see the world in black and white. The situation can only be either good or bad. There is no middle ground and no gray area. This means that if you're not perfect, then you're a failure. If something does not give you everything, then it's worth nothing. When we polarize, we think in extremes. However, life and people rarely work like that. Polarizing may make us focus on labeling something so much that we miss objectively seeing the good. For example, in your goal to be the top athlete in a tournament, you may see winning a silver medal as worthless simply because it's not the gold medal that you were aiming for. You miss out on celebrating what's worth celebrating: Your hard work, the journey, and how far you've come.

Countering Negative Self-Talk

Now that you've learned what to look out for and how you can identify negative self-talk as soon as it starts, you can learn how to stop it before it gets worse and completely take over. No matter how bad your self-talk is, you can always turn negative thinking into positive thinking. It does take time and practice, but your mean inner critic can be tamed and even booted out! Aside from talking to yourself as if you were talking to a friend, here are some tips on how you can practice thinking in a more optimistic way:

Become mindful of how you talk to yourself. Becoming more aware of our negative thinking patterns and how we let them impact our moods or actions is the first step toward change. One way to practice this is by taking note of your thoughts. Journal, schedule a daily reflection time, or type it in your phone's Notes app. Write down the thought, then ask yourself what could possibly be driving it, as well as how you feel about it. Then, ask yourself how you could possibly look at the situation in a better light. Laughter is the best medicine, so if you could also look at your thoughts in a humorous light, or if you could make light of your irrational beliefs, that might help make your inner voice sound more positive.

Challenge your negative thoughts. Once you're better at identifying negative thinking patterns, it's time to practice challenging your negative thoughts. This is where you'll try to look at the situation objectively and lay out the facts. Is there concrete evidence to support your thinking? If there is none, consider that you may be holding an irrational belief.

Talk it out. Sometimes, the best way to challenge negative self-talk is to actually verbalize it to someone. When you're not alone and when you're talking out loud, it becomes more difficult to be so mean to yourself because you hear just how irrational and unkind you're being. So, lean on your support systems. Call a loved one, schedule a catch-up session with your best friend, or talk to a therapist.

Put it on a shelf. It's important to face ourselves head-on, but sometimes it can get extremely overwhelming. During such times, it can be unproductive to feel your feelings, so it's alright to take a break and step away for a bit. It helps if you visualize taking the negative thought or belief you have and putting it away on top of a shelf or inside a box to be revisited later. This act can temporarily free you from overwhelming emotions and can even help give you a moment of clarity. Remember to revisit them, however, at a time that best suits you as we already know the negative effects of repressed emotions. You can choose to revisit your thoughts later that night as you're journaling or maybe even later in the week with your therapist.

Focus on the present moment. We know how effective mindfulness is in managing negative rumination. It provides a sense of relief, as well as the ability to pause and refocus. Remember the mindfulness techniques you learned. Breathe, ground yourself, meditate; let your mind wander, then focus on the present thought and the present moment. Then, let it go.

Ways To Improve Self-Talk

There are a lot of benefits you can get from practicing positive self-talk. Mainly, positive self-talk stops us from dwelling on the negatives and helps us cope during difficult times. Other potential benefits according to research are: A stronger immune system, reduced stress and pain levels, better heart health, improved physical and mental health, better self-esteem, and increased energy. Positive self-talk has also been linked to greater life satisfaction and a longer life. It's unclear exactly how positive self-talk is so good for us, but one theory is that it simply reduces the effects of stress on our bodies. Another theory is that optimistic people are more hopeful and, therefore, take better care of themselves (Waters, 2021).

Fortunately, there are ways to improve self-talk and you are already familiar with them! Keeping a gratitude journal, avoiding comparison, using positive affirmations, surrounding yourself with positive people, taking care of yourself, moving your body, visualization, and getting clear with your goals are just some of the most effective ways that can help improve your mindset and, therefore, improve your inner monologue (Karjala, 2020).

Remember that how we talk to ourselves does impact our actions, so it's important to work on it. Weave positive self-talk or reflection into your daily routine to help you practice and try befriending your mean inner critic. When it starts to shout pessimistic thoughts, try asking it questions and comforting it. Use the techniques you learned in chapter one.

Replacing the Word "Should" in Your Vocabulary

I *should* have done this; I *should* have done that. I *should* have been this, I *should* have been that. Sounds familiar? How many times have you used the word "should" recently? How many times have you used it in just the last hour? We squeeze so much into our schedules and have so many versions of ourselves for everyone, that we often feel guilty whenever we fall short. However, when we overload ourselves with responsibilities and commitments, we aren't exactly setting ourselves up for success. Therefore, we *are* bound to fall short.

That's when the term "should" starts showing up in our self-talk. "*I should have said this*," or "*I should have responded better*," or "*I should have given more.*" It's almost automatic. Something bad happens and our impulse is to think about what should have been. Now, recall the times this has happened to you and answer this: Where do those thoughts ever lead us? The answer is nowhere! It's not as if dwelling on 'what should have been' ever fixed the present situation. No! Instead, it only leads to self-blame and regrets. Should is the word could dipped in shame. It leads to unhealthy self-judgment. That's why it's important to try and replace the word "*should*" in our vocabularies. This is another effective method of improving self-talk.

Here's a way you can start doing it: Replace the word should with could or might. For example, if you are having a relaxing Sunday morning, instead of thinking, "I should be cleaning the house" simply say, "I might clean the house." You get to decide how to spend your time. If you hear yourself saying "I should have said 'this'", instead think "I could have said 'this'." That's how you can change your internal narrative and take the self-judgment out of the thought.

·♥·♥·♥·♥·♥·

Self-Talk Story You Need to Learn from Today

After becoming paralyzed at the age of 18, Paralympic Gold Medalist, Mallory Weggemann struggled with the weight of her own negative self-talk combined with her internalization of the judgments of others. "I allowed all of those limiting ideas to impact how I saw myself and even more so, what I perceived my worth to be," she says.

Mallory found the courage to look at herself in the mirror and remember that she was strong, she was resilient and she was brave. She not only survived the changes life had brought, but she also thrived to her wildest dreams. She encourages everyone to take pause and to focus on the words that you use with yourself, on the story that you tell yourself.

Her shared message is "*The positivity that exists within you comes from an understanding that true fulfillment is found in living a life of purpose and holding onto the faith that good overcomes.*" (Waggemann, 2021)

Chapter Activity: Change Your Vocabulary

We've learned so much about our inner voice and the importance of positive self-talk by now. Our words towards ourselves are just as important as our actions. We are now aware that it helps to replace the word "should" in our vocabularies, but that's not the only word we can avoid using. There are many other terms that make us feel bad about ourselves that we can do without. For this activity, we're going to identify exactly those words and we're going to create an action plan as to how we can replace them with something else or avoid using them altogether.

Get a pen and paper or you can use your phone's Notes app—whatever works for you as always! Then, list down the words or phrases your mean inner critic is always throwing at you. Right beside each one, write down how you can rephrase it in a more positive way. List as many as you can! You can add to the list every time you hear yourself use negative self-talk.

Here are some examples:

I will no longer say: "I'm a failure!"

I'll replace it with: "I'm a person who's growing and continuously improving."

I will no longer say: "I suck!"

I'll replace it with: "I'm still learning how to do/be…"

I will no longer say: "I can't do it!"

I'll replace it with: "I will figure out how to do it!"

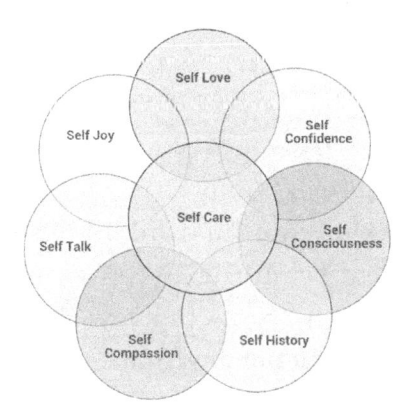

Attaining the Ultimate Self-Joy

We cannot cure the world of sorrows, but we can choose to live in joy. -Joseph Campbell

'Happiness' is such a beautiful word. It's also a beautiful feeling, maybe even the most beautiful. Everyone wants it. Everyone's looking for it. Everybody wants to know the secret to have it. In the Merriam-Webster dictionary (n.d.-c), happiness is officially defined as "a state of well-being and contentment." But what exactly is the key to achieving happiness? There's probably no "one secret formula." If there was one, we probably would have known that by now. However, what we do know is that self-understanding plays a key role. That's what we're going to discuss in this chapter.

None of us were born miserable, but a lot of us struggle with finding happiness in our lives. One main reason for this is that we view happiness as something that happens to us. What I mean is that we often rely on external factors to give us happiness—whether that's other people, our careers, money, or some type of goal we have yet to attain on the horizon. Sometimes, these things do make us happy. Oftentimes, they only do so temporarily, or they don't at all—*at least not in the way we expect them to make us feel*. Also, the expectation and subsequent disappointment when these external factors ultimately don't make us happy only make us more pessimistic.

As much as we want other people to make us happy, the truth is it is no one's responsibility to do that for us. The responsibility of making us happy relies solely on ourselves. Not one person owes us happiness, even the person we love most. And although it might seem cruel at first, it's actually not such a bad realization. What it actually means is that we are in control. It may seem daunting to think that you are on your own, but it also means that the power is within you. You don't have to look for happiness somewhere else, because you have it inside of you. Isn't that actually empowering and such a relief?

Self-Understanding Is the Key to Happiness

Still, I understand if you don't know where to start. Because to be able to practice self-joy, you have to know and understand yourself well first. That could be difficult, say, if you're not used to living on your own terms or if you haven't started on your self-love journey yet. No worries, I got you! Here are a few ways in which you can understand yourself better:

Declutter your mind. There are so many books and internet content nowadays telling us how we can achieve happiness or who we should be. And I get it, there are a lot of people who are seeking them out. That's you right now, and that used to be me! However, consuming too much advice from other people will only lead to confusion. Everyone is walking different paths in life, so your self-joy journey will also be completely unique to you. I'm not saying don't listen to advice but try to analyze the thought process behind it instead so that you can choose to retain only the ones that apply to you. That way, your brain won't get too tangled up in unnecessary ruckus, and you won't feel too overwhelmed. Remember, you're not trying to fit into other people's methods, no matter how tried and tested they claim it to be. Instead, you're trying to see which methods fit within your life. Then, you can use this knowledge to pave your own path and form your own opinions. So, if something isn't applicable to your journey, chuck it out—even if it came from this book!

A clear mind is a joy in and of itself, and it will help you hear your inner voice better.

Understand the bigger picture. Have you ever observed resilient people? Health care workers or parents, for example. Do you ever think, "If it were me, I wouldn't be able to do that day in and day out." Have you ever wondered how they do what they do even when it seems too difficult? Well, the answer is that they see the bigger picture! They understand their role and the purpose of their actions. The same is true in your self-knowledge journey. It's easy to get motivated in the beginning after reading a self-help book or two, but as mentioned, you will inevitably face challenges. You would have to confront difficult truths about yourself, and you would have to do the inner work, day in and day out. The only way you can keep up with it is if you focus on the bigger picture. And what is the bigger picture, you may ask? Well, it's simply understanding your true self! It's knowing who you are deeply so that you can steer your life in service to what brings you joy. Once you start understanding yourself and making choices based on what makes you happy, self-joy becomes a by-product, but before you get to that point, you would have to take it one day at a time, and some days might be more difficult than others. So, when you are tempted to quit, think of the bigger picture, and you'll see that tough times are just small bumps in the road.

Break it down. Sometimes, problems can seem so big and overwhelming that it's difficult to believe you'll ever feel joy again, or you can have so many beliefs about yourself that it's difficult to pinpoint exactly who you are. When this happens, take a step back and break the problem down into smaller and simpler pieces. Often, when faced with problems, we want to be rid of them immediately, so we look for instant solutions. However, self-understanding takes time. So, when you are faced with a big problem, remember that there is no instant way to fix it. Give yourself a chance to sit with the problem long enough, break it down into more easily understandable points, then start creating action plans. The more patience you have in dealing with a problem, the more effective your actions are. Write it all down; you'll get to know more about yourself in the process! It's in challenging times that we are able to see what we're made of.

Benefits of Self-Knowledge

What exactly are we aiming to know about our own selves? Basically everything! But to break it down, you're trying to get a good grasp of your personality traits, overall disposition, mental and emotional responses, needs, goals, preferences, physical characteristics, motivation, and abilities, as well as how you are within your relationships with other people. When we know these things about ourselves, it's easier to understand why we behave the way we do, or what behaviors we act upon that are not truly aligned with who we are.

Continue using the technique of thinking of yourself as a friend. The more we know about a friend, the better we understand their emotions and actions. For example, you might believe that you thrive better at work when put in a team environment, so you constantly volunteer to join a group project, but once you're in the middle of it, you wonder why it actually drains you. In this example, your self-knowledge may be lacking, which is what is leading you to put yourself in situations that actually don't align with who you are. Remember, you can be good at something and still have that something be unaligned with your core. To live a truly authentic and fulfilling life, self-knowledge is essential. Having an accurate representation of your true self will help you make better choices that don't sacrifice your values and your personality. For example, knowing who you are and what you stand for will help you choose better friends or partners. It will help you choose career paths that you truly enjoy or find meaningful. This leads to happiness—which you gave to yourself! Aside from self-knowledge being the catalyst for self-joy, it comes with other great benefits such as:

Less inner conflict and better decision-making. Is this for me? Is this not for me? Is this the right choice? Should I have done something else? These are the kinds of questions we plague ourselves with when we don't have a clear understanding of who we are. As we gain more self-knowledge, we pace back and forth doubting our every move less. That's because when you know who you are, the choices you need to make become clearer to you. Therefore, you don't torment yourself too much with inner conflict about what to do or not to do, or about what's right or wrong for you.

Self-control and resistance to social pressure. When you know yourself, you are in control! You are less likely to care about impressing others, hence, you will rarely succumb to social pressure. If you are the type of person who always has trouble saying "no," working on your self-knowledge can help with that. Also, when you know who you truly are, you are less likely to behave in ways that don't align with your values and beliefs. Self-knowledge is like an inner compass that always points you toward your true north.

Tolerance and understanding of others. The more you practice self-understanding, the better you become at identifying your strengths and weaknesses. The more you do so, the less likely you are to expect perfection from yourself, and this disposition extends to others too. Because you are aware that you are flawed, you understand that others are too. Therefore, you will be more empathetic—or tolerant at least—of other people's weaknesses, mistakes, or limitations.

Vitality and pleasure. In your journey towards self-knowledge, you will begin to identify the things that bring you energy and pleasure. Once you learn what they are, you are able to make choices towards them and eliminate those that don't bring you as much joy. Because of this, you are less likely to be overwhelmed by wanting to do everything. Doing things that bring you joy helps you feel more alive and helps make life more pleasurable and exciting.

V.I.T.A.L.S of Happiness

Now that we know that self-knowledge plays a key role in achieving happiness, let's further break it down to the six building blocks of the self. Thankfully, there's a useful acronym to help us remember:

V.I.T.A.L.S, which was created by counselor and author, Meg Selig. V.I.T.A.L.S stands for (Selig, 2016):

Values. One important component of the self, if not the most important, is our values. What motivates us? What moves us into action? What do we personally hold in high regard? Having worthwhile values and knowing them can help us make better life choices. It helps us look forward to just being alive, as well as gives us resilience and motivation, especially when times are tough. Some examples of values are "helping others," "being creative," or "practicing self-love." If you ever want to self-motivate, start identifying your values. Write them down on paper! Research has shown that simply jotting your values down motivates an individual to set goals and start taking action toward them (Falk et al., 2015).

Interests. Of course, we're not who we are without our unique interests! This includes our passions, hobbies, or anything that makes us pay attention for a long period of time. To know your interests, you can ask yourself some questions. What do you willingly pay attention to? What topic or activity draws out your curiosity? What concerns you? Our interests help us enter a sustained-focus mental state, which not a lot of activities do. For example, if art is one of your interests, you might be able to focus on painting for hours and hours. Some people even compare this mental state to what is experienced during yoga or meditation. Overall, having interests is not only what makes us interesting, but also what makes our lives more vivid and worthwhile.

Temperament. In our previous example, we talked about how you may excel at one thing, so you seek it out, but then have that one thing drain you. For example, you may seek out working in a group because you're good at being a team member, yet you feel drained by the end of the group activity. This could have something to do with your temperament, which describes our inborn preferences. Being an introvert or extrovert falls within this category. If you're an introvert, you restore your energy by being alone. Whereas extroverted people feel most energetic when they are with other people. Temperament also covers whether you're a planner or more of a go-with-the-flow type of person, as well as whether you make decisions more on the basis of logic or emotions. Most of the time, when we don't have a good grasp of our temperament, we try to change ourselves and make ourselves fit into situations that don't really accommodate us. Understanding your temperament is important because it allows you to show up just as you truly are and reduces your need to change yourself.

Around-the-clock activities. This refers to biorhythms, which is our internal unique clock that tells us what times during the day we like to do things. For example, it seems like every piece of advice on how to be successful tells us to start our day before the sun rises. While that might work for some people, it's not going to work for everyone. Also, success definitely doesn't depend only on being a morning person. Knowing your body's innate inclinations will help you make better decisions. You don't have to force yourself to wake up at 4 a.m. if you feel more energetic and productive at 5 p.m.! You could really just be a night person, and there's nothing wrong with that. In every area of life, it's much easier if you don't waste unnecessary energy trying to change who you are to fit a certain mold.

Life mission and meaningful goals. Earlier, we discussed how important it is to look at the bigger picture. Joy is fleeting and happiness comes and goes, but life goes on. It can be difficult to deal with the day-to-day if you are not sure what you are striving for. That's why it's important to be on the lookout for life missions or meaningful goals. It doesn't have to be just one, and you are also allowed to change your mind about them. You also don't have to have an answer right now. Still, as you go through life, remember to ask yourself, "What have been the most meaningful moments of my life so far?" You may gain valuable insight from your answer, and that might push you towards a new life goal that you are currently unaware of.

Strengths. This not only includes your skills, talents, or abilities. It also includes your character strengths such as empathy, love of learning, emotional intelligence, loyalty, fairness, curiosity, and more. Being aware of your strengths—and weaknesses—is one of the major components of self-love and self-confidence. You can play to your strengths when you know what they are. Likewise, when you know what you're not good at, you can choose to work on them or simply make them a smaller part of your life.

It's important to highlight that you should continuously reflect and try to understand yourself because you are constantly changing. The person you are today is not the same person you were yesterday. And in five or 10 years, you might be a completely different person. So, don't forget to check on your V.I.T.A.L.S periodically and always be true to YOU!

Finding Passion and Purpose

We've just talked about how important it is to have life missions and meaningful goals. Finding your passion or purpose in life is a big part of that. However, I understand that it's easier said than done. Some people figure out what theirs are during childhood, while others spend most of their life in search of one. Both of those are okay, one is not better than the other. As long as you are on the lookout for your passion and purpose, you are not wasting time! And you always have time; it's never too late to act upon things that make you feel most fulfilled. Because having passion and purpose leads exactly to that: Personal fulfillment. With that comes true joy and happiness.

But first, let's talk about passion and purpose. These words are often used interchangeably, but how are they different from each other? Let's start with *passion*. Passion is defined in the Merriam–Webster dictionary (n.d.–e) as the "intense, driving, or overmastering feeling or conviction." Passion is what brings emotions, motivations, and pleasure out of us. It is usually connected to our innate talents, desires, or abilities. To find your passion, simply look at what you love doing without feeling pressured to do it and without feeling stressed. Passion can be a great motivator for success. Most successful people have a great passion for their field. That's because, when you have passion for something, you will feel the innate pull to strive towards its mastery or you will simply enjoy doing it so much that you inevitably improve.

In that way, passion boosts productivity, which in turn can boost confidence and lead to success. Passion is what pulls us through tough times because we know that the endeavor itself is worth it.

Purpose, on the other hand, is the reason why we do what we do. Its official definition in the Merriam-Webster dictionary (n.d.-f) is "an action in the course of execution." It's the goal on the horizon, the reason we keep going forward. Unlike passion, which is connected to our innate talents and abilities, our purpose is connected to an understanding of our reason for living. It's what makes our unique background, life story, and desired future make sense to us. Purpose helps give us direction and keeps us focused. It is often the true yardstick for measuring our life's success. When you have a purpose, life becomes less of an experiment. You will be able to confidently move forward with conviction and clarity.

In short, passion is the "what" of your life, while purpose is the "why." Passion can burn out over time, and we can have different passions throughout our life. Purpose, however, usually lasts a lifetime. Purpose actually precedes passion, but passion is often easier to determine because it's more expressive. An example of a purpose is "to help as many people as I can learn to love themselves," and one of the passions that can come from that is "writing about self-love." Imagine passion as fire and purpose as what fuels it.

Still, we must learn how to bring passion and purpose together in order to achieve a more authentic and joyful life. So, how do you do that? Here are some questions you can ask yourself to get started on figuring out your passions:

What activities give me joy?

Which subjects am I most interested in or eager to learn about?

If money wasn't an issue, what job can I volunteer to do for a long time?

If I didn't have responsibilities, how would I spend my days?

What am I good at that I do willingly and happily?

What activity puts me "in the zone?"

As discussed, purpose precedes passion, so there's a reason why you like doing what you like doing. Once you're done with the above questions, you can ask yourself the following questions to get to your purpose:

Why was I given this gift or talent?
Why does this come easy to me while other things are a struggle?
Why do these issues bother me while others don't?
Why am I experiencing this in life?
What do my past and present experiences say about my future?

Try not to be too hard on yourself if you can't answer all of the questions and can't figure it all out right now. Figuring out your passion and purpose requires some deep soul searching, so it also requires deep self-knowledge. On the other hand, if you were able to figure out your passion and purpose, you may be wondering how to connect the two together. There are practical ways to do so, such as:

Continuously examine your life. In every stage of your life, you can choose to re-examine yourself and your journey. Constant soul-searching helps you determine your true passions and purpose, and it helps you find ways to connect the two. Take time out of your busy schedule and give yourself a little retreat. Journaling also helps. Whatever makes you look inward and reflect on your life is what we're after.

Begin to live with conviction. Once you've figured out where your passion lies, you can't just sit on that knowledge. It's all for naught if it doesn't inspire some sort of action from you. Now that you know what you want to do and who you are, begin to live every day with conviction. Let your passion and purpose reflect how you spend your time, what you consume, what you talk about, and what you devote yourself to. Make choices that keep you in the direction of your newfound conviction.

Redirect your passion to support your purpose. As previously discussed, your purpose is the 'why' of everything you do. You might have spent your life using your abilities and energy on the wrong things—things that do not align with your purpose. So, once you figure out what your purpose is, you have to redirect your passion to support it.

Embrace new opportunities. Opening ourselves up to new opportunities is the only way we grow. You might currently be living your life in ways that do not represent your true passion and purpose at all. For example, your career. You may not have to quit everything, but it's important to be on the lookout for opportunities that can help you better express your true passion and purpose.

Be bold enough to make major life adjustments. Once you have the knowledge and conviction, it's time to make some changes! For example, you might decide to leave a career path you've spent years on in exchange for one that is more aligned with your passion and purpose. Once you find your passion and purpose, your whole life may change if you let it. I hope you are brave enough to embrace these changes because it leads to living life on your own terms. You may have to go through a challenging transition, but the reward is a life that is more impactful, meaningful, and fulfilling. Remember, there is no price that is too much to pay for the kind of life you truly deserve. I hope you get the courage to break out of systems where you don't truly belong.

Learning How to Prioritize Your Happiness

When we talk about happiness, we sometimes make it seem like it's something that is on the horizon; something that needs to be grasped. And in some ways, it is. For example, figuring out your passions and purpose does give you happiness, as well as achieving goals, or simply becoming a better version of yourself. What needs to be given more spotlight, however, is the fact that happiness can also be found in the present moment. Happiness is actually all around us and inside of us! It only requires a slight mental shift to start believing that happiness is a direct result of our actions. Therefore, we don't have to wait around for happiness to come to us. We can learn how to do things every day that give us happiness. However, this requires us to stop doing things that do the opposite. For example, if you spend all your weekend binge-watching Netflix because that's what your whole family does, but you'd rather spend time moving your body, go move your body instead. Excuse yourself and go for a short walk. Start replacing activities that don't energize you with those that do or start making decisions based on what you want rather than what others want. For example, if the whole family is ordering pizza for dinner, but you don't really feel like eating pizza at the moment, order or cook yourself something else. The more you choose yourself—no matter how others may react—the more happiness you generate. Also, it results in more self-knowledge because you'll be able to see what happiness looks like for you. Then, you can decide more in favor of those things in the future.

Another way of increasing happiness in your day-to-day life is to find an interesting or playful way to do mundane tasks. For example, cleaning our space is extremely important in taking care of ourselves, but it's not always fun. Whenever you feel bored or find a task highly tedious, try doing it in a more interesting way. Maybe put on an upbeat playlist as you're cleaning or make it into a game where you get a reward in the end. This way you not only get stuff done, but you also have fun in the process.

Lastly, learning to embrace the present moment is also a path toward happiness. When you focus on the present, you begin to realize that you are not defined by your thoughts. It becomes more difficult to succumb to negative thinking when you develop an awareness and an appreciation of the *now*. Becoming more present also helps eliminate procrastination, and it snaps you out of living life on "autopilot" mode wherein you simply go through the daily motions of life without actually engaging your full consciousness. As we have discussed, being more mindful has many psychological benefits. It also helps empower us to set healthy boundaries with others and frees us from worrying too much about the past or the future.

Remember, every decision you make leads either towards or away from your happiness, so try to choose the path that leads towards it every chance you get.

Activities for Self-Joy

Your happiness is in your hands, so choose to give it to yourself as much as you can. Now that you know the importance of prioritizing your happiness not just in the long run, but also in your daily life, here are some practical things you can do every day to help you practice self-joy:

Laughter therapy. This non-pharmacologic approach is non-invasive, cost-effective, and easily implementable. All you need is yourself. Plus, there's only one step: Let out a laugh! Research shows that laughing, even fake laughter, can help improve mood, as well as reduce stress and anxiety (Akimbekov & Razzaque, 2021). So, an easy way to practice self-joy every day is to take five to 10 minutes of your time and just have a laugh.

Watch the sunrise or sunset. Aside from laughter, a simple and easy way to practice self-joy is to watch either the sunrise or the sunset. Research has shown that this activity helps boost our moods, improve sleep, and reduce inflammation and depression symptoms (Pedersen, 2022). So, take a walk outside around the time the sun rises or sets, watch the sky change colors, and marvel at its beauty.

Listen to a song you love. We've all experienced being deeply moved or energized by music. Studies have shown that listening to music has a lot of benefits such as reduced anxiety and lower blood pressure, as well as improved sleep quality, mood, memory, and focus. Music is also effective in jump-starting creativity (John Hopkins Medicine, n.d.). So, take some time out every day to listen to a song you love. You can even blast the speaker as you're doing a mundane task to make the activity more joyful.

Take a vacation or plan a trip. Nothing guarantees a good time better than taking a vacation! Traveling somewhere new has been shown to potentially have a lot of mental health benefits such as enhanced empathy, focus, and energy (Crowne, 2013). If time and resources are preventing you from going on your dream vacation at the moment, you can act as a tourist within your hometown instead. Go someplace you haven't been to before or try out a new restaurant. Instead of going to places you always frequent, break your routine and explore something new. Or you can daydream about your upcoming vacation! Research has shown that even just planning a vacation makes us substantially happier (Kumar et al., 2014). Just the anticipation of taking a trip has been shown to bring us joy—much more so than shopping does! So, even if you don't have the means to travel yet, open up that spreadsheet, research about the places you would like to visit and look into what food you'd like to try—yum!

Make a note of the things you are grateful for. We already know the power that comes with gratefulness. Being grateful allows us to be more mindful, and being present opens us up to more joy. It also helps us redirect our focus from the negatives to the positives. So, add to your gratitude journal every day, or schedule a few minutes within your day to simply give thanks.

Help someone. One effective way of giving yourself joy is by giving it to others. When you volunteer your time and energy for other people, it reminds you that there's more to life than just yourself and that your actions do matter and can brighten someone else's day. There's even research that shows that people who willingly help others are more satisfied in life compared to those who don't. It was also observed that they were less vulnerable to negative emotions (Espinosa et al., 2022). So, volunteer in your local shelter, lend a friend a helping hand, or simply do something nice for someone.

Think about your loved ones. During tough times, it's easy to feel alone. When this happens, shift your thoughts towards your loved ones. When was the last time you laughed with them, and what was it about? Just simply thinking about how connected we are to other people helps remind us that we are not alone and that we have people who care about us. You can even take it one step further by actually reaching out to them, whether it's via call, email, or text. Studies have shown that making an effort to connect with a loved one helps elevate our mood, reduce stress levels, and even boost our overall physical health (Pathways Home Health and Hospice, n.d.). So, call up a loved one and have a quick chat. It may make your day better and vice versa!

Move your body. We already know the benefits of getting enough physical activity, so if you're feeling a little down, try to do some stretching, jumping, or maybe go out for a quick walk. Moving our bodies help release hormones associated with calmness and happiness. If you need a quick fix, stand up and do a couple of jumping jacks. You will feel lighter and happier almost immediately afterward.

· ♥ · ♥ · ♥ · ♥ · ♥ ·

Self-Joy Story You Need To Learn From Today

Let me tell you a story. There was once a rich and successful woman. She had all the riches she could ask for, yet she was always anxious and restless. She decided to seek out a therapist to talk to. When the woman finally met with her therapist, she shared her problem. She said that she has no shortage of anything, but she was always worrying.

The therapist told the woman to come back the following day and that she would teach her how to be happy. The following day, the woman saw the therapist looking around for something outside of her office. She asked how she could help, and the therapist replied, "I have lost my ring."

After hearing this, the woman started looking around for the therapist's ring too. They searched for a long time with no success. Then, the woman decided to ask for more details. "Where did your ring fall exactly?" she said.

"Inside my office," the therapist responded calmly. "But it's very cluttered in there, so I decided to look outside."

Of course, the woman was surprised at this answer. She exclaimed, "If your ring fell in the office, then why are you looking outside? How will you find it outside when it's inside?"

The therapist simply smiled at her. Then, she declared that this was the solution to the woman's problem. The therapist said: "You came with the problem that you have no shortage of anything; but still, you are not happy with your life. Happiness is right there inside you, but you are looking for it outside in the materialistic world."

She then added, "The entire ocean is inside you, but you are looking for water outside with a spoon."

The woman was enlightened and motivated to reflect on her life. From then on, she strived to find happiness within herself (inspired by Invajy, 2022).

Chapter Activity: Five Minutes of Joy Every Day

When you choose to find joy in each day you increase your sense of self - leading to fulfillment, happiness, and self-joy. The goal of this activity is to choose to feel good each and every day - for at least five minutes. Make joy part of your routine - you don't need to finish your chores or check everything off your to-do list first. If making joy a priority is not easy for you, start small. Make a list of all the little things that make you smile. The things that bring you peace. The things that make you happy.

Everybody has five minutes.

Here are a few examples:

1. Take up knitting. The beauty of knitting is you can stop and start as your life allows.

2. Enjoy a hot drink! Really take time to savour it.

3. Dance crazily to your favorite song. Go wild - no one's watching.

4. Do a puzzle. One piece or ten, you can take your time and still get that feeling of joy and accomplishment.

5. Hula Hoop! Do somersaults! Twirl for no reason other than you can.

6. Sit outside in the sunshine and soak up some vitamin D.

7. Spend time with your pet - walk your dog, play with your cat.

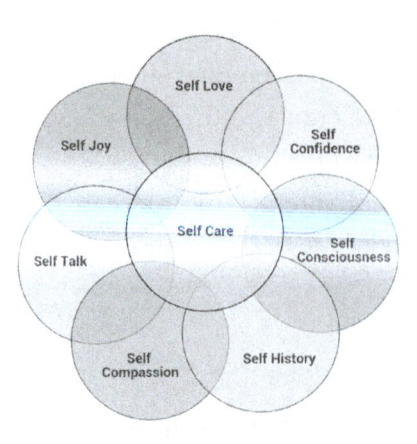

Conclusion

Love is a powerful emotion. It pushes us and sustains us. It helps us connect with others and with the world. It makes us do magnificent things. It's necessary for our survival. Psychologists say that out of all of the emotions we hold, love is the most profound, intense, and life-changing. We have so much capacity within us to love others. Imagine if we direct the love we have towards ourselves instead. How life-changing would that be? The answer is *extremely*! Self-love is the key to a more fulfilling and authentic life, and every woman deserves to have that.

Now that you know about the 7D self-care framework, I encourage you to take the lessons you have learned and apply them to your life. Start by recognizing and acknowledging your worth, and then make a conscious effort to prioritize your own needs and desires. Remember that each aspect of the framework takes practice so be kind to yourself and speak to yourself with love and compassion. It's time to let go of negative self-talk and self-doubt and embrace your true self. Take the steps necessary to cultivate a healthy relationship with yourself, and watch as your relationships with others also improve. I challenge you to make self-love a priority in your life and to inspire others around you to do the same. It's worth it, I promise.

If this book helped you in some way and you think it can also help other women, please consider leaving a review on Amazon, Barnes &

Noble, Lulu, or wherever you purchased your copy from. This will help the book get recommended to other people who are on a similar journey. The more people this book reaches, the more it may be of help. Let's create a world where women empower each other to embrace their unique beauty and worth. Because women are amazing and worthy of love. *You* are amazing and worthy of love. It's about time you knew that. It's about time you loved yourself!

♥ · ♥ · ♥ · ♥ · ♥

References

Cambridge Eating Disorder Center. (n.d.). *Eating disorder facts*. Cambridge Eating Disorder Center. Retrieved May 7, 2023, from https://www.eatingdisordercenter.org/facts-figures/

Akimbekov, N. S., & Razzaque, M. S. (2021). Laughter therapy: A humor-induced hormonal intervention to reduce stress and anxiety. *Current Research in Physiology, 4*, 135-138. https://doi.org/10.1016/j.crphys.2021.04.002

Ardrey, T. (2023, April 8). *This Atlanta plastic surgeon explains why it's not the end of "the BBL era" despite social media hype*. Insider. https://www.insider.com/surgeon-things-need-to-know-about-trendy-bbl-reduction-lift-2022-12#:~:text=Data%20from%20The%20Aesthetic%20Society

Asghar, A. (n.d.). *The science of self-love: the evidence-based benefits of loving yourself*. Ness Labs. https://nesslabs.com/self-love#:~:text=Self%2Dlove%20can%20lead%20to

Barrie, J. M. (1987). *Peter Pan*. Penguin.

Becker, M. (2023, May 4). *The story of Hanna: How self-compassion can foster healthy relationships*. Center for Mindful Self-Compassion. https://centerformsc.org/the-story-of-hanna-how-self-compassion-can-foster-healthy-relationships/

Better Health Channel. (2023, February 16). *Body image - women.* Betterhealth.vic.gov.au. https://www.betterhealth.vic.gov.au/health/healthyliving/body-image-women

Be Well Stanford. (2019, August 2). *The benefits of self-forgiveness.* Scope Blog Stanford. https://scopeblog.stanford.edu/2019/08/02/the-benefits-of-self-forgiveness/#:~:text=Research%20has%20shown%20that%20those

Breines, J. G., & Chen, S. (2012). Self-compassion increases self-improvement motivation. *Personality and Social Psychology Bulletin, 38*(9), 1133-1143. https://doi.org/10.1177/0146167212445599

Brooks, A. W. (2014, June). *Get excited: Reappraising pre-performance anxiety as excitement.* Harvard Business School. https://www.hbs.edu/faculty/Pages/item.aspx?num=45869

Butler, K. (2014, September). *Why BMI is a big fat scam.* Mother Jones. https://www.motherjones.com/politics/2014/08/why-bmi-big-fat-scam/

Callahan, A. (2021, May 18). *Is B.M.I. a scam?.* The New York Times. https://www.nytimes.com/2021/05/18/style/is-bmi-a-scam.html

Cambridge Dictionary. (n.d.). Shapewear. In *Cambridge Dictionary.* Retrieved May 9, 2023, from https://dictionary.cambridge.org/us/dictionary/english/shapewear

Campbell, J. (2008). *The hero with a thousand faces.* Barnes & Noble (2nd ed.). New World Library.

Cash, T. (1990). *The psychology of physical appearance: Aesthetics, attributes, and images.* APA PsycNet. https://psycnet.apa.org/record/1990-98350-003

CDC. (2022a, March 31). *New CDC data illuminate youth mental health threats during the COVID-19 pandemic.* Centers for Disease Control and Prevention. https://www.cdc.gov/media/releases/2022/p0331-youth-mental-health-covid-19.html

CDC. (2022b, April 6). *Preventing child abuse & neglect.* Centers for Disease Control and Prevention. https://www.cdc.gov/violenceprevention/childabuseandneglect/fastfact.html

CDC. (2022c, June 3). *Defining adult overweight and obesity.* Centers for Disease Control and Prevention. https://www.cdc.gov/obesity/basics/adult-defining.html#:~:text=Adult%20Body%20Mass%20Index&text=If%20your%20BMI%20is%20less

Chen, K. (2022, April 22). *New data shows emotional abuse increased among teens during pandemic.* Healthier, Happy Lives Blog. https://healthier.stanfordchildrens.org/en/data-shows-emotional-abuse-increased-among-teens-during-pandemic/

Cherney, K. (2020, June 22). *Cold shower for anxiety: Does it help?.* Healthline. https://www.healthline.com/health/anxiety/cold-shower-for-anxiety#research

Cherry, K. (2020, November 21). *Why body positivity is important.* Verywell Mind. https://www.verywellmind.com/what-is-body-positivity-4773402

Children's Wisconsin. (n.d.). *Contributing factors to abuse and neglect.* Childrenswi.org. Retrieved May 15, 2023, from https://childrenswi.org/childrens-and-the-community/community-partners-professionals/child-abuse-prevention/prevent-child-abuse-wisconsin/information-and-statistics/contributing-factors

Christensen, J. (2022, December 27). All around the world, women are better empathizers than men, study finds. *CNN.* https://edition.cnn.com/2022/12/26/health/empathy-women-men/index.html

Cohen, R., Newton-John, T., & Slater, A. (2017). The relationship between Facebook and Instagram appearance-focused activities and body image concerns in young women. *Body Image, 23,* 183-187. https://doi.org/10.1016/j.bodyim.2017.10.002

Coles, N. A., Larsen, J. T., & Lench, H. C. (2019). A meta-analysis of the facial feedback literature: Effects of facial feedback on emotional experience are small and variable. *Psychological Bulletin, 145*(6). https://doi.org/10.1037/bul0000194

Compton, E. (2018, March 2). *Intuitive eating: The non-diet is the best diet.* Sph.umich.edu. https://sph.umich.edu/pursuit/2018posts/intuitive-eating.html

Cosmopolitan India. (2020, September 9). *10 Women Share Their Inspiring Self-Love Stories.* Cosmopolitan India. https://www.cosmopolitan.in/celebrity/features/g21601/10-women-share-their-inspiring-self-love-stories

Crowne, K. A. (2013). Cultural exposure, emotional intelligence, and cultural intelligence. *International Journal of Cross Cultural Management, 13*(1), 5-22. https://doi.org/10.1177/1470595812452633

Cuddy, A. J. C., Wilmuth, C. A., & Carney, D. R. (2012). The benefit of power posing before a high-stakes social evaluation. *Harvard Business School, 13*(027). https://dash.harvard.edu/handle/1/9547823

Czepczor-Bernat, K., Kościcka, K., Gebauer, R., & Brytek-Matera, A. (2017). Ideal body stereotype internalization and sociocultural attitudes towards appearance: a preliminary cross-national comparison between Czech, Polish and American women. *Archives of Psychiatry and Psychotherapy, 19*(4), 57-65. https://doi.org/10.12740/APP/78172

Davis, T. (n.d.). Self-consciousness: *Definition, examples, & tips to overcome it.* Berkeley Well-Being Institute. https://www.berkeleywellbeing.com/self-consciousness.html

Do Something Org. (n.d.). *11 facts about body image.* DoSomething.org. https://www.dosomething.org/us/facts/11-facts-about-body-image#fn2

Doherty, K., & Schlenker, B. R. (1991). Self-consciousness and strategic self-presentation. *APA PsycNet*, 1-18. https://psycnet.apa.org/doi/10.1111/j.1467-6494.1991.tb00765.x

Dreisbach, S. (2011, February 3). *Shocking body-image news: 97% of women will be cruel to their bodies today.* Glamour. https://www.glamour.com/story/shocking-body-image-news-97-percent-of-women-will-be-cruel-to-their-bodies-today

Elsig, C. M. (2022, January 24). *The dangers of suppressing emotions*. The CALDA Clinic. https://caldaclinic.com/dangers-of-suppressing-emotions/

Espinosa, J. C., Antón, C., & Grueso Hinestroza, M. P. (2022). Helping others helps me: Prosocial behavior and satisfaction with life during the COVID-19 pandemic. *Frontiers in Psychology, 13*. https://doi.org/10.3389/fpsyg.2022.762445

Eugene Therapy. (2020, October 29). *10 tips to overcome self-doubt*. Eugene Therapy. https://eugenetherapy.com/article/overcome-self-doubt/

Exley, C. L., & Kessler, J. B. (2019). The gender gap in self-promotion. *National Bureau of Economic Research*. https://doi.org/10.3386/w26345

Fab UK Magazine. (2018, March 16). Over 30% of teenage girls feel unattractive when they are not wearing makeup. *Fab UK Magazine*. https://fabukmagazine.com/over-30-of-teenage-girls-feel-unattractive-when-they-are-not-wearing-makeup/

Falk, E. B., O'Donnell, M. B., Cascio, C. N., Tinney, F., Kang, Y., Lieberman, M. D., Taylor, S. E., An, L., Resnicow, K., & Strecher, V. J. (2015). Self-affirmation alters the brain's response to health messages and subsequent behavior change. *Proceedings of the National Academy of Sciences, 112*(7), 1977-1982. https://doi.org/10.1073/pnas.1500247112

Flegal, K. M., Kit, B. K., Orpana, H., & Graubard, B. I. (2013). Association of all-cause mortality with overweight and obesity using standard body mass index categories. *JAMA, 309*(1), 71-82. https://doi.org/10.1001/jama.2012.113905

Geva, S., & Fernyhough, C. (2019). A penny for your thoughts: Children's inner speech and its neuro-development. *Frontiers in Psychology, 10*. https://doi.org/10.3389/fpsyg.2019.01708

Gilbert, L. K., Breiding, M. J., Merrick, M. T., Thompson, W. W., Ford, D. C., Dhingra, S. S., & Parks, S. E. (2015). Childhood adversity and adult chronic disease. *American Journal of Preventive Medicine, 48*(3), 345-349. https://doi.org/10.1016/j.amepre.2014.09.006

Gillen, M. M. (2015). Associations between positive body image and indicators of men's and women's mental and physical health. *Body Image, 13,* 67-74. https://doi.org/10.1016/j.bodyim.2015.01.002

Goldstein, J. M., Seidman, L. J., Horton, N. J., Makris, N., Kennedy, D. N., Caviness, V. S., Faraone, S. V., & Tsuang, M. T. (2001). Normal sexual dimorphism of the adult human brain assessed by in vivo magnetic resonance imaging. *Cerebral Cortex, 11*(6), 490-497. https://doi.org/10.1093/cercor/11.6.490

Good Therapy. (2019, June 17). *Self-compassion.* Goodtherapy.org. https://www.goodtherapy.org/learn-about-therapy/issues/self-compassion

Gotter, A. (2017, June 25). *Self-conscious emotions.* Healthline. https://www.healthline.com/health/self-conscious-emotions#complications

Gotter, A., & Raypole, C. (2023, February 14). *Considering EMDR therapy? What to expect.* Healthline. https://www.healthline.com/health/emdr-therapy#effectiveness

Gruys, K. (2019, May 1). *How does appearance affect our success?.* University of Nevada Reno. https://www.unr.edu/nevada-today/news/2019/atp-appearance-success

Gupta, S. (2022, September 4). *How to embrace self-acceptance.* Verywell Mind. https://www.verywellmind.com/self-acceptance-characteristics-importance-and-tips-for-improvement-6544468#citation-3

Heinström, J. (2010). *Internal locus.* Science Direct. https://www.sciencedirect.com/topics/computer-science/internal-locus

Hinde, N. (2017, December 15). *10 women share powerful stories of self-love.* HuffPost UK. https://www.huffingtonpost.co.uk/entry/in-your-skin-women-share-their-journey-of-self-acceptance_uk_5a33b29de4b01d429cc7cdf6

Holland, T. (2018, April 28). *Facts about touch: How human contact affects your health and relationships.* Dignityhealth.org.

https://www.dignityhealth.org/articles/facts-about-touch-how-human-contact-affects-your-health-and-relationships

Huber, S. (2019, September 24). *8 important tools for healing trauma.* Thrive Global. https://community.thriveglobal.com/8-important-tools-for-healing-trauma/

Huecker, M. R., Shreffler, J., McKeny, P. T., & Davis, D. (2023, January). Imposter phenomenon. *PubMed.* https://pubmed.ncbi.nlm.nih.gov/36251839/#:~:text=Imposter%20syndrome%20(IS)%20is%20a

Huntington, C. (n.d.). *Body positivity: Definition, quotes, & tips.* The Berkeley Well-Being Institute. Retrieved May 7, 2023, from https://www.berkeleywellbeing.com/body-positivity.html

Illinois Childhood Trauma Coalition. (n.d.). *Look through their eyes.* Lookthroughtheireyes.org. https://lookthroughtheireyes.org/how-can-i-identify-it/

Institute For Advanced Psychiatry. (n.d.). *Signs you may be dealing with lingering effects of childhood trauma.* Psychiatryfortworth.com. Retrieved May 15, 2023, from https://www.psychiatryfortworth.com/blog/signs-you-may-be-dealing-with-lingering-effects-of-childhood-trauma

Invajy. (2022, July 6). *Inspirational stories about life – happiness is within you (story #27).* Invajy.com. https://www.invajy.com/happiness-story/

IT Cosmetics & Eranos. (2021). *Women's Confidence Report.* Women's Confidence. https://womensconfidence.report/#localresults

Janson, M. (2011, December 2). *Self-compassion eases the pain of a divorce.* Greater Good. https://greatergood.berkeley.edu/article/item/self_compassion_eases_the_pain_of_a_divorce

Jin, A., & Whittall, I. (2022, August 29). *A look at South Korean plastic surgery.* HMSR. https://www.hmsreview.org/issue-7/2022/8/a-look-at-south-korean-plastic-surgery

John Hopkins Medicine. (n.d.). *Keep your brain young with music.* Hopkinsmedicine.org. Retrieved May 20, 2023, from https://www.hopkinsmedicine.org/health/wellness-and-preventi on/keep-your-brain-young-with-music#:~:text=Research%20has %20shown%20that%20listening

Karim, F., Oyewande, A., & Abdalla, L. (2020). Social media use and its connection to mental health: A systematic review. *Cureus, 12*(6). https://doi.org/10.7759/cureus.8627

Karjala, T. (2020, January 31). *The power of positive self-talk.* Forbes. https://www.forbes.com/sites/forbescoachescouncil/2020/01/31/t he-power-of-positive-self-talk/?sh=cde805a3a154

Kate, G. (2021, May 16). *Positive self talk quotes & sayings.* The Goal Chaser. https://thegoalchaser.com/positive-self-talk-quotes/

Kaziga, R., Muchunguzi, C., Achen, D., & Kools, S. (2021). Beauty is skin deep; the self-perception of adolescents and young women in construction of body image within the Ankole society. *International Journal of Environmental Research and Public Health, 18*(15), 7840. https://doi.org/10.3390/ijerph18157840

Kids Helpline. (2023, April 21). *Understanding child emotional abuse.* Kids Helpline. https://kidshelpline.com.au/parents/issues/understanding-child-emotional-abuse

Kuehn, K. (2022, January 24). *40 body positive quotes everyone should read.* Reader's Digest. https://www.rd.com/article/body-positive-quotes/

Kumar, A., Killingsworth, M. A., & Gilovich, T. (2014). Waiting for merlot: Anticipatory consumption of experiential and material purchases. *Psychological Science, 25*(10), 1924-1931. https://doi.org/10.1177/0956797614546556

Kurdieh, I. (2019, November 22). *How I overcame my childhood trauma.* Medium. https://medium.com/@internalworlds/how-i-overcame-my-child hood-trauma-f44eb81fed36

Laurell K. Hamilton. (2007). *Mistral's Kiss*. Penguin Random House Canada. https://www.penguinrandomhouse.ca/books/74323/mistrals-kiss-by-laurell-k-hamilton/9780345443618

Li, P. (2023, April 26). *Keys to a happy childhood according to science*. Parenting for Brain. https://www.parentingforbrain.com/happy-childhood/

Locket, E. (2019, August 30). *Grounding: Exploring earthing science and the benefits behind it*. Healthline. https://www.healthline.com/health/grounding#types

MacPherson, R. (2022, February 23). *What is diet culture?*. Verywell Fit. https://www.verywellfit.com/what-is-diet-culture-5194402#:~:text=Diet%20culture%20s%20the%20pervasive

Martin, C., Herrick, K., Sarafrazi, N., & Ogden, C. (2018, July). *Data briefs - number 313 - July 2018*. Centers for Disease Control and Prevention. https://www.cdc.gov/nchs/products/databriefs/db313.htm

Merriam-Webster. (n.d.-a). Comfort zone. In *Merriam-Webster.com*. Retrieved May 4, 2023, from https://www.merriam-webster.com/dictionary/comfort%20zone#:~:text=noun

Merriam-Webster. (n.d.-b). Forgiving. In *Merriam-Webster.com*. Retrieved May 17, 2023, from https://www.merriam-webster.com/dictionary/forgive

Merriam-Webster. (n.d.-c). Happiness. In *Merriam-Webster.com*. Retrieved May 19, 2023, from https://www.merriam-webster.com/dictionary/happiness#:~:text=%3A%20a%20state%20of%20well%2Dbeing

Merriam-Webster. (n.d.-d). Narcissist. In *Merriam-Webster.com*. Retrieved May 16, 2023, from https://www.merriam-webster.com/dictionary/narcissist

Merriam-Webster. (n.d.-e). Passion. In *Merriam-Webster.com*. Retrieved May 20, 2023, from https://www.merriam-webster.com/dictionary/passion#:~:text=%3A%20a%20strong%20liking%20or%20desire

Merriam-Webster. (n.d.-f). Purpose. In *Merriam-Webster.com*. Retrieved May 20, 2023, from https://www.merriam-webster.com/dictionary/purpose

Merriam-Webster. (n.d.-g). Self-consciousness. In *Merriam-Webster.com*. Retrieved May 10, 2023, from https://www.merriam-webster.com/dictionary/self-consciousness

Merriam-Webster. (n.d.-h). Self-doubt. In *Merriam-Webster.com*. Retrieved May 11, 2023, from https://www.merriam-webster.com/dictionary/self-doubt

Merriam-Webster. (n.d.-i). Self-love. In *Merriam-Webster.com*. Retrieved April 29, 2023, from https://www.merriam-webster.com/dictionary/self-love

Morgado, F. F. da R., Betanho Campana, A. N. N., & Fernandes Tavares, M. da C. G. C. (2014). Development and validation of the self-acceptance scale for persons with early blindness: The SAS-EB. *PLoS ONE, 9*(9), e106848. https://doi.org/10.1371/journal.pone.0106848

National Today. (n.d.). *Self-love day*. National Today. https://nationaltoday.com/self-love-day/#:~:text=In%20ancient%20Greece%2C%20self%2Dlove

Nationwide Children's. (n.d.). *Physical abuse*. Nationwidechildrens.org. https://www.nationwidechildrens.org/conditions/physical-abuse-trauma

Neff, K. (n.d.). *Self compassion*. Self-Compassion Org. Retrieved May 16, 2023, from https://self-compassion.org/the-three-elements-of-self-compassion-2/

Neff, K. (2015, September 30). *The five myths of self-compassion*. Greater Good. https://greatergood.berkeley.edu/article/item/the_five_myths_of_self_compassion

NHS. (2023, January 27). *Spotting signs of child sexual abuse.* Nhs.uk. https://www.nhs.uk/live-well/spotting-signs-of-child-sexual-abuse/

Nishizawa, S., Benkelfat, C., Young, S. N., Leyton, M., Mzengeza, S., de Montigny, C., Blier, P., & Diksic, M. (1997). Differences between males and females in rates of serotonin synthesis in human brain. *Proceedings of the National Academy of Sciences, 94*(10), 5308-5313. https://doi.org/10.1073/pnas.94.10.5308

NSPCC. (n.d.). *Neglect.* NSPCC. Retrieved May 15, 2023, from https://www.nspcc.org.uk/what-is-child-abuse/types-of-abuse/neglect/

Ortiz-Ospina, E. (2019, September 18). *The rise of social media.* Our World in Data. https://ourworldindata.org/rise-of-social-media#:~:text=Facebook%2C%20the%20largest%20social%20media

Parisi, D. (2022, April 21). *How new brands are reconciling the contradiction of "body-positive shapewear".* Glossy. https://www.glossy.co/fashion/how-new-brands-are-reconciling-the-contradiction-of-body-positive-shapewear/

Pathways Home Health and Hospice. (n.d.). *The true benefits of caring for our loved ones.* Pathways Home Health and Hospice. Retrieved May 20, 2023, from https://pathwayshealth.org/hospice-topics/the-true-benefits-of-caring-for-our-loved-ones/#:~:text=It

Paulise, L. (2023, March 8). *75% of women executives experience imposter syndrome in the workplace.* Forbes. https://www.forbes.com/sites/lucianapaulise/2023/03/08/75-of-women-executives-experience-imposter-syndrome-in-the-workplace/?sh=11fee456899a

Pedersen, T. (2022, August 29). *10 benefits of watching the sunrise.* Psych Central. https://psychcentral.com/health/watching-the-sunrise#Recap

Peterson, T. (2022, March 25). *What is self-confidence?*. Healthyplace.com. https://www.healthyplace.com/self-help/self-confidence/what-is-self-confidence#:~:text=Anneli%20Rufus%20(2014)%20asserts%20that

Plackett, B. (2021, June 15). Do you have an inner voice? Science can't agree if everyone does. *Discover Magazine*. https://www.discovermagazine.com/mind/do-you-have-an-inner-voice-science-cant-agree-if-everyone-does

Prevent Child Abuse America. (n.d.). *Child sexual abuse prevention*. Prevent Child Abuse America. Retrieved May 15, 2023, from https://preventchildabuse.org/what-we-do/child-sexual-abuse-prevention/#:~:text=Specifically%2C%20nearly%201%20in%204

Psychology Today. (2022, June 21). *Trauma-focused cognitive behavior therapy*. Psychology Today. https://www.psychologytoday.com/us/therapy-types/trauma-focused-cognitive-behavior-therapy

Raes, F. (2010). Rumination and worry as mediators of the relationship between self-compassion and depression and anxiety. *Personality and Individual Differences, 48*(2010), 757-761. https://doi.org/10.1016/j.paid.2010.01.023

Ranganathan, V. K., Siemionow, V., Liu, J. Z., Sahgal, V., & Yue, G. H. (2004). From mental power to muscle power--gaining strength by using the mind. *Neuropsychologia, 42*(7), 944-956. https://doi.org/10.1016/j.neuropsychologia.2003.11.018

Rasmussen, K. R., Stackhouse, M., Boon, S. D., Comstock, K., & Ross, R. (2019). Meta-analytic connections between forgiveness and health: the moderating effects of forgiveness-related distinctions. *Psychology & Health, 34*(5), 515-534. https://doi.org/10.1080/08870446.2018.1545906

Reille, A. (2020, September 22). *Irene's story: From self-doubt to self-confidence*. Thriving in Admin. https://thrivinginadmin.com/blogs/2020/9/22/irenes-story-from-self-doubt-to-self-confidence#

ReportBuyer. (2018, August 22). The global compression wear and shapewear market size is expected to reach $6.4 billion by 2024, rising at a market growth of 5.8% CAGR during the forecast period. *PR Newswire*. https://www.prnewswire.com/news-releases/the-global-compression-wear-and-shapewear-market-size-is-expected-to-reach-6-4-billion-by-2024--rising-at-a-market-growth-of-5-8-cagr-during-the-forecast-period-300700919.html

Runfola, C. D., Von Holle, A., Trace, S. E., Brownley, K. A., Hofmeier, S. M., Gagne, D. A., & Bulik, C. M. (2012). Body Dissatisfaction in Women Across the Lifespan: Results of the UNC-SELFand Gender and Body Image (GABI) Studies. *European Eating Disorders Review*, 21(1), 52-59. https://doi.org/10.1002/erv.2201

Sansom, W. (2023, January 5). *Treatment for combat-related PTSD advances with method shown to be fast, effective.* UT Health San Antonio. https://news.uthscsa.edu/treatment-for-combat-related-ptsd-advances-with-method-shown-to-be-fast-effective/

Selig, M. (2016, March 9). *Know yourself? 6 specific ways to know who you are.* Psychology Today. https://www.psychologytoday.com/us/blog/changepower/201603/know-yourself-6-specific-ways-know-who-you-are

Seppala, E. (2013, June 26). *Are women more compassionate than men?.* Greater Good. https://greatergood.berkeley.edu/article/item/are_women_more_compassionate_than_men

Shin, S. H., Lee, S., Jeon, S.-M., & Wills, T. A. (2015). Childhood emotional abuse, negative emotion-driven impulsivity, and alcohol use in young adulthood. *Child Abuse & Neglect*, 50, 94-103. https://doi.org/10.1016/j.chiabu.2015.02.010

Solis-Moreira, J. (2023, January 23). *6 ways to practice self-love.* Forbes Health. https://www.forbes.com/health/mind/how-to-practice-self-love/

Stanborough, R. J. (2020, November 25). *What to know about a negative body image and how to overcome it.* Healthline.

https://www.healthline.com/health/negative-body-image#signs-and-symptoms

Stanford News. (2018, February 1). Matching neglected children with foster care families earlier in life promotes resilience, healthy functioning, new Stanford study says. *Stanford News*. https://news.stanford.edu/2018/02/01/foster-care-helps-neglected-children-resilient-healthy/

Stanford, F. C., Tauqeer, Z., & Kyle, T. K. (2018). Media and its influence on obesity. *Current Obesity Reports, 7*(2), 186-192. https://doi.org/10.1007/s13679-018-0304-0

Substance Abuse and Mental Health Services Administration. (2023, March 17). *Understanding child trauma*. Samhsa.gov. https://www.samhsa.gov/child-trauma/understanding-child-trauma

Sutton, M. (2019, July 16). *Meet the inspiring women who've worked hard at loving their bodies - and want you to do the same*. Good Housekeeping. https://www.goodhousekeeping.com/uk/lifestyle/a28292672/body-positivity-stories-how-to-love-your-body/

Tagle, A., & Schneider, C. M. (2022, January 4). *Diet culture is everywhere. Here's how to fight it*. NPR.org. https://www.npr.org/2021/12/23/1067210075/what-if-the-best-diet-is-to-reject-diet-culture

Tomiyama, A. J., Hunger, J. M., Nguyen-Cuu, J., & Wells, C. (2016). Misclassification of cardiometabolic health when using body mass index categories in NHANES 2005-2012. *International Journal of Obesity, 40*(5), 883-886. https://doi.org/10.1038/ijo.2016.17

Truu, M. (2022, January 2). The really old, racist, and non-medical origins of the tool we use to measure our health. *ABC News*. https://www.abc.net.au/news/2022-01-02/the-problem-with-the-body-mass-index-bmi/100728416

U.S. Department of Veterans Affairs. (2022, November 9). *Cognitive processing therapy for PTSD*. Ptsd.va.gov.

https://www.ptsd.va.gov/understand_tx/cognitive_processing.asp#:~:text=Cognitive%20Processing%20Therapy%20(CPT)%20is

Virginia Department of health. (n.d.). *Self-acceptance*. Virginia.gov. Retrieved May 8, 2023, from https://www.vdh.virginia.gov/workforce-wellness/wellness-topics/self-acceptance/

Waters, S. (2021, June 9). *The power of positive self talk (and how you can use it)*. Better Up. https://www.betterup.com/blog/self-talk

Weggemann, M., & Weggemann, M. (2021). I'm a Paralympic Gold Medalist, Here's How I Use Positive Self-Talk To Boost My Confidence. *Well+Good*. https://www.wellandgood.com/mallory-weggemann-positive-self-talk/

Weingus, L. (2017, February 2). *7 reasons running improves confidence*. Mindbodygreen. https://www.mindbodygreen.com/articles/why-running-improves-confidence

West, M. (2022, April 29). What to know about the body positivity movement. *Medical News Today*. https://www.medicalnewstoday.com/articles/body-positivity

Whitener, S. (2021, April 7). *Anxiety vs. relaxation: Relabeling anxiety as excitement*. Forbes. https://www.forbes.com/sites/forbescoachescouncil/2021/04/07/anxiety-vs-relaxationrelabeling-anxiety-as-excitement/?sh=268docd97afd

Whitman, W. (2006). *Leaves of grass*. Simon & Schuster Paperbacks.

Williams, D., Happé, F., & Jarrold, C. (2008). Intact inner speech use in autism spectrum disorder: evidence from a short-term memory task. *Journal of Child Psychology and Psychiatry, 49*(1), 51-58. https://doi.org/10.1111/j.1469-7610.2007.01836.x

Williams, N. (2022, June 29). Screen time and mental health. *News-Medical.net*.

https://www.news-medical.net/health/Screen-Time-and-Mental-Health.aspx#:~:text=Recent%20studies%20have%20found%20many

Winner Spirit. (2022). *Focus on your path - motivational speech (Simon Sinek)*. Youtube.com. https://www.youtube.com/watch?v=OL__TF_x5uw

Wolpert, S. (2007, April 3). Dieting does not work, UCLA researchers report. *UCLA*. https://newsroom.ucla.edu/releases/Dieting-Does-Not-Work-UCLA-Researchers-7832

Woods, R. F. (2018, August 31). *14 benefits of practicing acceptance*. Psych Central. https://psychcentral.com/blog/cultivating-contentment/2018/08/14-benefits-of-practicing-acceptance#4

Zarse, E. M., Neff, M. R., Yoder, R., Hulvershorn, L., Chambers, J. E., & Chambers, R. A. (2019). The adverse childhood experiences questionnaire: Two decades of research on childhood trauma as a primary cause of adult mental illness, addiction, and medical diseases. *Cogent Medicine, 6*(1). https://doi.org/10.1080/2331205x.2019.1581447

Printed in Great Britain
by Amazon